HURRICANE HARVEY:
RESCUE TO RESTORATION

How One City Came Together To Fight The Flood Of The Century

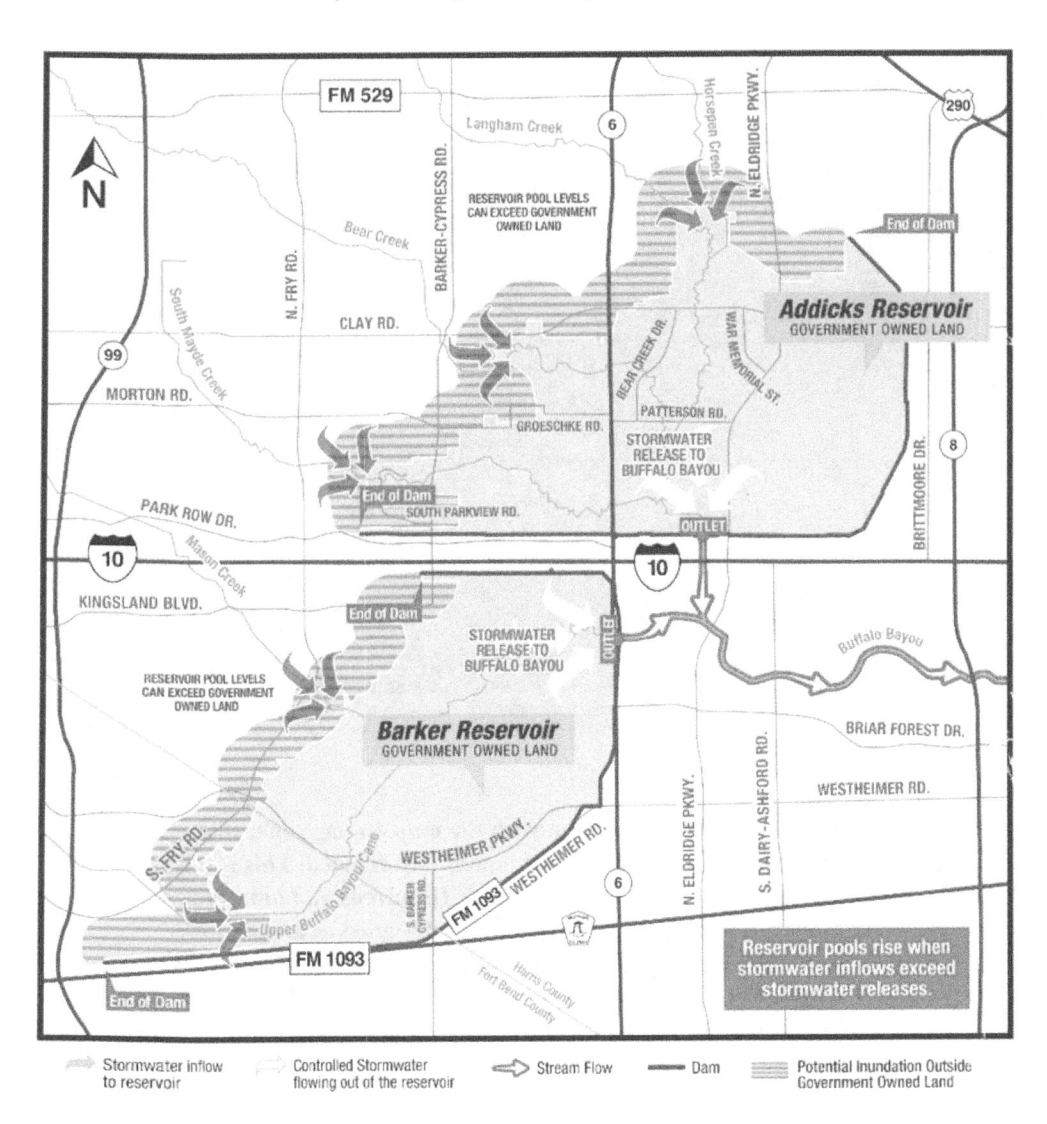

All rights reserved. No part of this publication may be reproduced, stored in a retrieval system, or transmitted in any form or by any means, electronic, mechanical, photocopy, recording or otherwise, without the prior written consent of the publisher.

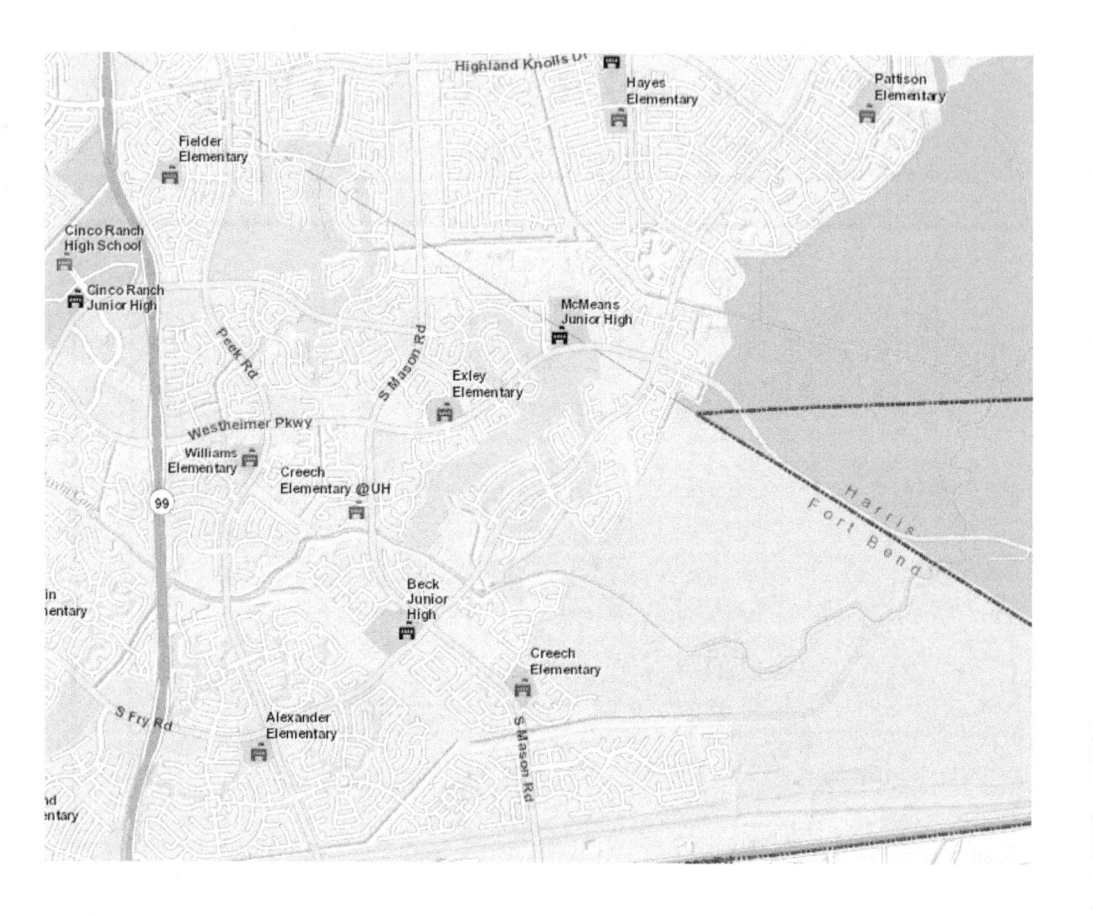

When you compare this map with the map on page one, you will see why Katy and West Houston had homes that flooded. This is the far southwest corner of the map on page one. Hundreds and hundreds of homes on this map are in the area that is designed as areas where "Reservoir Pool Levels Can Exceed Government Owned Land." This land was designed to hold reservoir overflow if we experienced a 500 or 1,000 year flood event. Harvey was a 1,000 year event.

To interact with others around our Harvey experience, please join us on Facebook at *Hurricane Harvey: Rescue to Restoration*

SATURDAY

AUGUST 26, 2017 - Calm Before The Storm

Hurricanes are a way of life for those who live along coastal Texas. Every year, we have hints of catastrophic events that are hyped by the news media to be "the Apocalypse to end all Apocalypses."

The preliminary rains from Harvey had been falling for a couple of days as we headed to a local restaurant for a nice dinner. Long time Houstonians, we cracked jokes at the restaurant about another dud of a hurricane. I could still remember the craziness of Rita in 2005, when millions of people evacuated the greater Houston area. My parents got stuck in the parking lot that Interstate 45 became while trying to get to Dallas from Houston. After being on the road for over ten hours and almost out of gas, they finally made it to shelter. I rode the storm out at our house and had it significantly easier than the vast majority of those who evacuated.

Despite my bravado, I am well aware of the destructive possibilities of hurricanes. Earlier in 2005, I helped turn a church in south Houston into a shelter during Katrina. We hosted people who came out of New Orleans. I remember driving to the Astrodome to pick up families who were sheltered there. They told stories of walking for miles out of the city with only the clothes on their backs. One family that we helped looked like they had escaped out of a war zone. They literally slept for 24 hours when they finally got to the shelter.

Sure it was raining in Katy, Texas, but all the predictions of wind, rain, and destruction were just another hyped story for a slow news cycle. Little did we know, but the biggest flood event in the last 1,000 years was about to hit our community with a vengeance!

SUNDAY
AUGUST 27, 2017 - From Bad to Worse

Every devastating hurricane has its own unique footprint. For Irma, it was its sheer power and magnitude. For Katrina, it was the lethargic response to the tragedy, both public and government. For Harvey, it was the simple fact that it never moved! Harvey sat over us and dumped trillions of gallons of water on southeast Texas in a three day period.

Harvey was the "Perfect Storm" for the greater Houston area. Rivers in the area were already trying to handle water from massive rains in North Texas earlier in the month. The Addicks and Barker reservoirs, constructed in the 1940's as the last line of defense for Houston against floodwaters, were filled up from prior rains in the area. The Brazos River to the west of Katy was flowing at historic levels. On top of this, Harvey dropped over 40 inches of rain in three days, an unprecedented deluge that would have overwhelmed any coastal city.

As you look at the map on page one (Addicks Reservoir (A) is north of Interstate 10, Barker Reservoir (B) is south of Interstate 10), notice the area in the Barker Reservoir labeled "Reservoir pool levels can exceed government owned land." That area represents thousands of homes in Katy!

Early Sunday morning, August 27 I received a text from our Lead Pastor Jerry Edmonson that services were cancelled. As the Groups Pastor at The Fellowship, we had talked the day before about Sunday services and, as conditions worsened overnight, Jerry made the decision to cancel them. If you know anything about churches, rarely are Sunday morning services cancelled. This definitely wasn't a good sign!

I put this up on Facebook and headed out to heed my own advice:

Just a reminder to all my friends: we have an awesome government and helping agencies (police, fire, rescue, National Guard). BUT they are a last resort when you are in an emergency. If water is rising around you and you think you are gonna get trapped in, get to higher ground! Make sure you can drive out of where you are. I'm checking my exit routes, you might check yours. Just a little neighborly advice.

Clearly, things had significantly deteriorated overnight. My parents live on the northwest side of the Addicks Reservoir, just outside of the overflow area. I knew they hadn't left yet, so I drove up to see how things looked. As I drove it was a progressive revelation that this was really bad. On Fry Road, just north of Interstate 10 there was a usually empty bayou (South Mayde Creek) that was almost flowing over the four lane road. By the time I got to their house, I was convinced my parents needed to go to Waco to stay with my sister. Dad, with memories of his ordeal being stuck in traffic from Hurricane Rita, gave me the, "I'll think about it" response, which in Dad speak means "Heck NO!" I asked him what his plan was if things got worse. He said, "If it gets bad, I'll just drive down Morton Road all the way to the Grand Parkway/99 and head to Waco." It sounded reasonable, but as I left I decided to see how Morton Road looked towards the Grand Parkway/99. Within about two miles, it was impassable! I called Dad back and said, "you gotta head out now!" He said "I'll think about it" and ended up riding out the entire storm.

Leadership Lesson #1 - Leaders know that the best information is obtained by seeing IT for yourself! You don't get what you expect you get what you inspect!

On the way back home, I had an incredible God sense that this storm was going to be really bad AND that I needed to put myself in a position to help people. That would definitely mean NOT being stuck in my home without the ability to get through flooded streets. Driving home, roads which had been passable were closing as the waters continued to rise. Walking in the door, I quickly told my wife, Connie, "you've got 10 minutes and we have to go or we are going to be stuck!" Thankfully, she trusted me and we headed out to sleep at Carly and John's (our daughter and son-in-law) on an air mattress, in the living room, for the next three nights.

After we got settled at the apartment, I began networking with people at our church and other contacts who were either in need of rescue or interested in helping with rescues. In every catastrophic event, there is a distinct progression of response to the overwhelming disaster that takes place. In countries where people are left with resources and given freedom to think on their feet, the first response to a large scale emergency comes from average citizens with a passion to help one another. Next, the response is private citizens working with the government. The final phase of the response is when the government fully takes over.

In the initial phase, regular folks pitch in and do what it takes to help. Often, they work in conjunction with Government First Responders who are, honestly and simply, overwhelmed by the massive need. During Harvey, people who called 911 at this point in the flooding were put in a queue to wait for help — help that would have taken days to materialize if not for private citizens! Government First Responders were doing the best they could, but they simply don't have the personnel to respond to thousands of emergencies and rescues in a matter of hours.

Jenn, a member of The Fellowship, posted that Mike (her father), Damon, Ryan, and Kyle had two boats and were trying to get to Katy from North Texas to help with rescues. They needed road closure information and contact info for those needing rescue. At this point, I was getting texts and Facebook posts from people asking for help. Jenn and I began to coordinate this team getting to our area to help with rescues on Monday; something we hoped wouldn't be needed but KNEW would be needed if the rain didn't stop.

At this early stage of

My son in law Damon and I took our boat down to the Katy/Houston area to assist in the rescue efforts. We were accompanied by Damon's brother in law Ryan and friend Kyle who operated a second boat. We began in Katy and moved around as needed in West Houston and North near the Addicks and Barker dam area. Due to the response of all the volunteers arriving we continued moving to different locations as the need arose. This continued for three days as we moved to Vidor, Orange and Beaumont. I have shared some pictures and videos but none of the victims. Collectively we directly assisted about 75 people and 15 dogs. We were a very small part of a larger picture who assisted thousands in need. We received invaluable support and direction from my daughter in Katy and her church who deserve a lot more credit than us. We also had the support of a retired fire fighter from Orange and his father, who again quickly directed us to people in need.
We were all amazed at the civility and cooperation by all involved, including first responders, who were only concerned with removing people from the flood waters. I saw first responders from Tulsa to California.

Leadership Lesson #2 - Leaders don't underestimate the "little guy." People are the most underutilized and under tapped resource of any organization.

the hurricane, many of the makeshift shelters that had been established were filling to capacity. Churches were gearing up their response and so was Katy ISD. As an 8th Grade school teacher, I was on the email distribution that kept us informed of district level decisions. Thankfully, our Superintendent, Dr. Lance Hindt, and our school board had the courage to open school facilities as shelters. We were told that on Monday morning, Cinco Ranch and Morton Ranch High Schools would open to shelter citizens who were being flooded. We were also informed that schools would be closed for at least the entire WEEK (a clear sign that things were moving from bad to worse). Ultimately, students did not return to school until 9/11.

Rescues on Sunday shut down when it got dark; it was just too dangerous to be on flooded streets and yards in a boat in the dark. This was actually a pattern throughout my time assisting in Harvey. Working hard "doing" during the day and spending the night time networking and planning for the next day. I worked 15-18 hour days for the first ten days of Harvey.

While I didn't have a lot of details about Cinco Ranch High opening as a shelter, I figured that I would get there at 7:00 AM the next morning and see if I could help. At the least, I could be of some assistance given my experience setting up a shelter during Katrina. And it would definitely beat hanging around in the apartment twiddling my thumbs! The greater hope was that the rain would relent and people would not need to evacuate the next morning.

Leadership Lesson #3 - Leaders fully leverage social media. They realize it is the most cost effective, and sometimes simply the MOST effective way to communicate today.

MONDAY
AUGUST 28, 2017 - Shelter

Throughout the night, the rains continued. I arrived at Cinco Ranch High School at 7:00 AM expecting to see the beginnings of a shelter. What I found was a very capable Katy Police Officer, a couple of other volunteers, and about six or seven maintenance and cafeteria employees.

We began organizing as best we could. Intake would be inside the doors in the foyer, housing of evacuees in the cafeteria, and staging of supplies and donations in the rotunda and the hallways. I remember visiting with Superintendent Hindt and thanking him for his work and for opening our schools as shelters for those in our community (something many districts would not have undertaken).

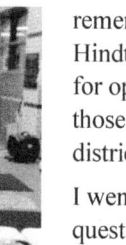

I went outside to help direct people, answer questions, and organize traffic flow. By 7:40 AM volunteers, evacuees, and donations began arriving at a brisk pace. Within a couple of hours, we had teams of people managing traffic, doing intake, helping evacuees get settled in the shelter, taking donations, sorting donations, and managing food preparation and distribution. As the rain poured, I was overwhelmed watching hundreds of people dive in to help any way they could. Ultimately, the outpouring of donations was so immense that we began routing donations to the 9th grade center at the other end of the school. By the end of the day, we filled that center with donations as well!

Leadership Lesson #4 - Leaders are convinced that the early bird really DOES get the worm. They show up early, ready to work!

During this Private Response to the disaster (remember I mentioned 3 stages of progression of response to a disaster: Private, Private/Government, Government), I was amazed to watch hundreds of people not directly impacted by the flooding give their time, talents, and resources to help their neighbors. It was a beautiful thing to watch!

By 1:00 PM, systems were developed and the shelter began to reach capacity (later in the afternoon Cinco Ranch Junior High was opened as a shelter as well and filled to capacity). By the end of the day we had over 600 evacuees sheltered at Cinco Ranch High School. We also helped hundreds of other evacuees connect with a place to stay. The school was an easy contact point for evacuees and those picking them up from all over Katy and Houston. Despite the rain and chill, it was heartwarming to watch person after person who came from a flooded home reunited with a friendly face.

As people stepped into leadership roles, I transitioned out of what I was doing to focus on helping with rescue operations. Because of my contacts through the church and the community, I was in the unique position to connect rescue boats (many from out of town) with those needing rescue.

I was especially concerned about a fellow teacher who was needing assistance getting out of their home in Canyon Gate. John (my son-in-law) and I decided to find the boat staging area to see if we could locate someone to help them. I had lost contact with the guys from North Texas, as they got into the water and began rescuing people.

MONDAY

AUGUST 28, 2017 - Rescue

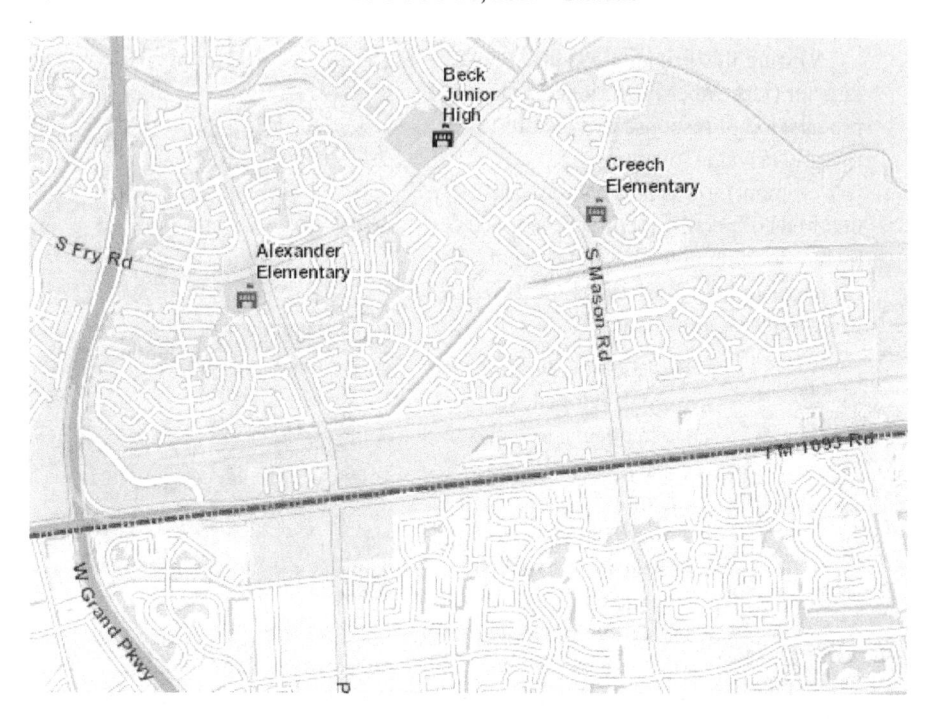

Around 2:30 PM, John and I headed to help my fellow teacher. As we pulled up the map on Google, it navigated us to Canyon Gate Subdivision. If you compare the map above (Canyon Gate is just south of Creech Elementary) with the maps on pages one and two, you will see that we were headed into one of the more devastated areas in Katy. In fact, the vast

majority of the approximately 720 homes in the subdivision were flooded during Harvey.

Very quickly, we found ourselves in the middle of controlled chaos on South Fry Road near Peek. Despite the fact that we were in a "tall tires" Jeep Wrangler that my daughter wisely bought in high school, (she and John had been married a little over a year and Carly was working on a Masters in Social Work through Baylor), we could not drive any further in the water.

I pulled into the parking lot in front of a donut shop I infrequently frequent. As we hopped out and walked to the intersection, we saw people unloading from high profile vehicles ("jacked up" jeeps and trucks, dump trucks, a few military vehicles). Many of the people were carrying backpacks or trash bags filled with what little they took out of their home. At this intersection, these evacuees got into vehicles like ours and were taken further up Fry Road (I found out later that night the Whole Foods at Grand Parkway/99 and South Fry was being used as a staging area for people coming out of the water to get picked up by friends and family). The high profile vehicles headed back into the flood waters east on South Fry Road.

John and I decided that he would stay at the intersection helping people and I would hop on one of the high profile vehicles headed deeper into the floods. I hitched a ride on a High Profile Vehicle to Beck Junior High. My goal was to find a boat and navigate it to my friends home.

The parking lot at Beck Junior High had about 10 boat trailers scattered around. They had developed a very thorough system. There were boats in the water dropping off evacuees coming north on Mason Road from Creech Elementary school. Shallow water boats were going back

Leadership Lesson #5 - Leaders ask a lot of open-ended questions and are not afraid to ask for help. They know that often you have not because you ask not!

into the neighborhoods and shuttling evacuees to Creech Elementary. Deeper draft boats were taking those evacuees to Beck Junior High. At Beck, high profile vehicles shuttled evacuees to the corner of Peek and South Fry. From there cars, Jeeps, and trucks took them to the Whole Food parking lot where they were picked up by friends and family. All of this had been organized by volunteers just jumping in and helping!

I helped a couple of boats unload evacuees and mentioned that I had an address for an evacuee and needed help getting them. One of the boat drivers said "hop on," so I got in the boat and we headed out.

I introduced myself to the two-man crew and almost fell out of the boat when the driver said his name was Damon. Damon was Jenn's brother-in-law I'd helped navigate to the area and texted with through the day giving him addresses! I tucked this experience in my memory as another Harvey "God thing"!

This was one of the first moments I'd had in the flood zone to really look around and take in what I was seeing. I was sitting in a boat going full throttle down Mason Road towards the Westpark Tollway . . . . in a boat! I just passed the auto repair shop where I got my car fixed . . . . . in a boat! As we got off Mason road, we navigated the side streets making our way to the address. Often, we had to get out and portage over low spots, but usually we were able to easily navigate the streets . . . . in a boat! As we neared the house, I saw my co-worker headed out in a different boat. Someone else had already rescued them! We decided to pick up some other evacuees and quickly had a boat full. We took them back to Beck Junior High and got them unloaded. I had to relieve myself and told the guys I'd be right back. When I got back to the loading area, they were gone! I chalked it up to the fluidity of emergency situations (you help people you will never see again, you work intimately with people that you won't recognize in three years, people say they will do things and because of changing circumstances they don't do them).

I hitched a ride on another boat back to Creech Elementary to see how I could help. There was a line of about 50 people in the gym waiting to get on a boat to go to Beck. A loading area was set up in the parking lot in chest deep water. People waited in the somewhat protected area of the school until a boat was available. I remember thinking, as I watched the water spreading across the wood floor, that the floors were going to be a total loss. My phone had died, so I borrowed a charger from someone there and got it charged a bit. I was getting worried about letting John know what was going on and found out he had already walked back to his apartment (a couple of

Leadership Lesson #6 - Leaders keep their phone charged! They know that good communication is VITAL to accomplishing anything! They know it also keeps those you work with engaged and empowered to make good decisions.

miles). The keys to the Jeep were in my pocket! Thankfully John is also forgiving in the "fluidity of emergency situations."

As darkness approached, boats began heading to Beck to load up for the night. I hopped on one of the boats and went back to Beck as well. While helping evacuees unload there, I realized that the reason boats were not taking people further up South Fry Road was because of the bridge. Bridges over the bayous in the area were a huge hindrance for rescue when the flooding happened! Boats like to stay on known routes (several times we drove OVER cars that were in the flood water as we were rescuing people). Bridges are high points where boats "bottom out" (drag on the ground). People who were dropped off at Beck had to get into very high profile vehicles to get over the bridge (think garbage truck or military transport vehicle). Here at Beck, there were three military vehicles and a few other vehicles carrying people to the intersection where I had left John.

I hopped on one of the last military vehicles headed away from the flood zone with a family of six evacuees (parents and teenagers). I struck up a conversation and one of them eventually asked me, "where are they taking us?" Their situation was so dire that they jumped in a boat with complete strangers, were ferried to a drop off, jumped in the back of a military vehicle with complete strangers, and thought they were being taken somewhere to stay! I told them most of the shelters were closed for the day (or full) and that this vehicle was taking them to another spot near the Grand Parkway/99 where someone could meet them. They got on their phones and began making calls to friends and family.

I climbed out at the intersection where the Jeep was parked and headed to the apartment. Carly and John live across the street from the church and I swung by the church to open the building for some citizen First Responders staying there that night. On the way, I stopped at an intersection next to a couple of guys pulling a boat. I invited them to stay at the church as well, so they followed me there.

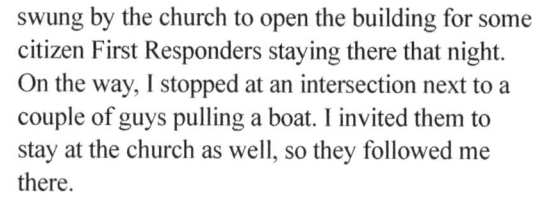

We found couches in the youth building for them to sleep on and they went with me to take a much needed shower at Carly's apartment. Although it was August in Houston, being soaking wet all day left a chill in the bones. In fact, my wallet got soaked through and I still have a dollar bill that ink bled into as a keepsake. I also have a nice scar on my knee where I hit a trailer hitch as we were loading boats onto trailers, in waste deep water, in the dark, at Beck Junior High.

Our long-time friends, Mark and Diane, came in from Dallas with their friend, Chris. They brought a U-Haul of supplies, an RV, and a boat. We got them settled at the church as well.

Carly, John, Connie and I talked about how we could help the next day. Pastor Jerry, at The Fellowship, emailed asking staff to meet at 10:00 AM Tuesday morning to discuss our response and possibly opening as a shelter. I finished the night touching base with some of the boat crews I was networking with and got some much needed sleep.

Leadership Lesson #7 - Leaders are the first ones up and the last ones to bed. Leading to make a difference often looks like obsession or "craziness" to others. Leading requires dedication, time, and energy!

TUESDAY
AUGUST 29, 2017 - Extraction Points

Through the night, we continued getting texts and Facebook messages from people wanting to evacuate. Early Tuesday morning, the rescuers at The Fellowship and our team of five folks headed out. The boats headed to the flood waters and the evacuation team arrived where I had been the previous night. We expected to see a fully developed extraction system. We went by the parking lot of the Whole Foods and there was nothing set up! We drove down to the intersection at South Fry and Peek and nothing was happening! Aaron (a fellow Pastor at The Fellowship) headed down to check on the boats at Beck. The rest of the team met in the parking lot of Alexander Elementary. It was a perfect extraction spot. The road was drivable from the Grand Parkway/99 all the way to the school. That eliminated the final step in the extraction process I saw yesterday. There would be no need to shuttle people back to Whole Foods.

As we stood around talking and evaluating the location, a Katy ISD police car pulled up. The window rolled down and the Katy Police Officer from Cinco Ranch High School, my fellow shelter builder, looked out the driver side window at me and said, "what are y'all up to?" We exchanged pleasantries and I told him we were thinking of setting the parking lot up as an extraction point for folks evacuating. He got on the phone for a minute, looked back at me and said, "the parking lot is yours" and drove off. That sure felt like another "God thing!"

We knew we would have to organize for vehicles bringing people out of the flooded area southeast of us and vehicles coming to pick people up from the northwest (Grand Parkway/99 and South Fry). We also knew that

15

Leadership Lesson #8 - Leaders make sure the right person is serving in the right spot! The wrong person in a key spot will destroy effectiveness!

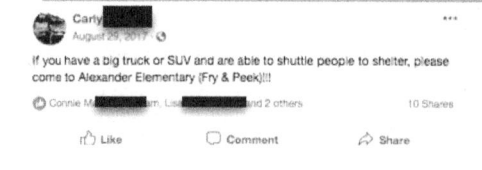

people would be coming out of the floods who had no place to go, so we began working with others at The Fellowship to transport them to shelters. We placed folks to direct traffic and I left Carly in charge to get things organized. John and I went to check on the boats, which were now in the water. Connie and Diane, our Dallas friend, were using social media and texting addresses and contact info of people needing evacuation to guys in boats.

There were two other locations in the area where boats were pulling people out of the water. One was around the corner from the church, just south on Mason near Westheimer Parkway. The other was in front of my middle school, McMeans, which was further east on Westheimer Parkway (almost to where Fry curves from south to west). John and I headed out to see what was going on at these other locations.

On Mason, we discovered that boats had launched at the bridge and people were being shuttled to an extraction point at the British Prep School just south of Westheimer Parkway. I left John there to help out as best he could and headed to The Fellowship to meet with our staff at 10:00 AM to discuss our response to Harvey.

The Fellowship is a church of about 1,000 people passionate about both proclaiming AND living out the gospel. We know the "Good News" we have to share is that Messiah Jesus came to this earth and took our sins upon Himself. We are dedicated to proclaiming that all who believe in Him do not have to work for forgiveness. Believing in Him brings forgiveness. We also believe that declaring the Good News of Jesus verbally goes hand in hand with demonstrating the love of Christ to others. In this meeting, it wasn't a question of whether we would respond to this disaster but HOW we would respond. Yes, we had staff members impacted and many of us were displaced, but we could NOT not respond!

We very quickly determined that we could best serve the community by doing four things. We could serve as a staging area for responders, rather than a shelter for evacuees. There

> Fellowship Staff.
>
> **Tomorrow is a new day.** A new day for the body of Christ to love our city. **We are going to keep our offices closed another day** and ask you to take care of your neighbors, rescue people from high water (great job Joey, Brian and Shannon – you guys are heroes), work at the shelters, Facebook the needs, pray for the recovery efforts and more. Just be the body of Christ. If you can make it up to the church safely then please join me for a conversation at 10:00 a.m. to discuss what it would take for The Fellowship to open as a shelter for the community. The need is increasing and the sheltering resources are currently limited. Come with your thoughts about what we need to do to make this happen.
>
> I want to thank all of you for all that you continue to do to help. I am sad to say that both Robert and Joe's homes flooded again along with many in our church family. I know others of you flooded or had to evacuate your homes with the possibility of flooding still looming. Our prayers and support are with you.
>
> So, if you can make it up to the church I'll see you at 10 a.m.
>
> Sharing the Gospel in 2017.
>
> Dr. Jerry Edmonson, Founding and Lead Pastor
> **The Fellowship** - www.thefellowship.org

were hundreds of people in the community, including the National Guard, who would be much better at their job if they had a cool place to sleep, warm showers, a great breakfast to start the day, and an awesome supper to end their long day. We realized we could store and distribute supplies and resources for those in need. Vast amounts of "stuff" was coming from all over the country to help and we could facilitate that distribution.

Since we weren't going to be a shelter, we determined we could best serve our flooded neighbors by asking our "not flooded" members and attendees to host evacuees in their homes. Most of our members have extra bedrooms and bathrooms. Rather than having evacuees sleeping on cots in the church and using the shower facilities at the YMCA across the street, why not just get them into homes?

Finally, since we were close to the epicenter of significant flooding, we could be a community rallying point for the area. Various staff members were assigned key roles. My role was to keep doing what I was doing, networking with boats in the water and helping bring evacuees to the church for assistance.

I left the meeting and checked on John. British Prep was still serving as an extraction point and I informed John that The Fellowship was going to mobilize to help folks get to the church and find host homes. I swung by to touch base with Living Word Lutheran Church at the corner of Mason and Westheimer Parkway. They had opened as a shelter. On the way out after visiting with the Pastor, I grabbed a piece of pizza and took a picture of myself to send to Damon and Kyle who were out doing rescues again today. Yesterday we had joked that we would love some pizza. I wanted to rub it in that I was enjoying hot pizza while they were in the water.

When I left there, I headed east on Westheimer Parkway towards McMeans to see what was happening in that flooded area. As I got near the middle school I teach at, I was amazed to see boats being dropped into the water in front of the school on Westheimer Parkway! I parked the Jeep because the water was too deep and walked to the school. There were various boats being unloaded into the water. Past the school, towards the neighborhood to the east, people were being dropped off by boats and walking west past the school carrying trash bags of their belongings.

As I surveyed the scene, I realize that the neighborhoods right around my school were severely impacted. I knew we didn't have any boats in the water in this location and asked who was in charge. I was directed towards a white truck where Bruce was busy on the phone and watching over the activities. I quickly exchanged info with Bruce to coordinate our efforts. He was from the Bellville area and usually had several boats working with him. Bruce seemed to be someone who knew what he was doing. He would prove to be a great contact in the future.

I worked my way back over to Alexander Elementary and was amazed at what was in place. Carly and the team had implemented a wonderful system. Diane and others were helping feed addresses and names of those needing evacuations to boats in the water. Others on the team were out managing traffic flow as hundreds of cars came into the area to pick up evacuees. Another team shuttled evacuees to The Fellowship for help.

Cars were slowly making their way from the Grand Parkway east on South Fry Road into the area. At one of the entrances into the school, high profile vehicles were transporting evacuees to the parking lot. As I looked over the system the only adjustment needed was moving traffic control onto South Fry

Leadership Lesson #9 - Leaders build systems that work and train people to work in the system who can train others in the system.

Road to help with traffic flow. I got out on the street with a couple of guys and showed them what we needed done. I was shocked that every 6th or 7th car coming to the area was an evacuee who wanted to see if their house was "okay." Information was unclear and very confused away from the flood zone. People weren't even aware that water was still rising and many of their neighbors who had not evacuated the day before were now evacuating!

After about 20 minutes of realigning the traffic flow, I grabbed someone driving up to volunteer and asked him to take my spot. I showed him what I was doing and told him that I had to go do something else. I told him he couldn't leave until he had trained someone to do what he was doing before he left.

Other thoughtful neighbors brought food and water. Carly was overwhelmed at one point by the simple act of someone bringing Chick-fil-A for the volunteers.

I left to check on other extraction points. At British Prep things were winding down and John was no longer needed. We headed to McMeans and found that boats were being loaded onto trailers as dusk approached.

At The Fellowship, various staff and volunteers were in full swing mobilizing the community and developing systems to accomplish the vision outlined in the morning meeting. The entire facility was being used. Donation drop off, storage, and organizing was happening in the Children/Youth Building. Volunteer sign up, evacuee assistance, and logistics was developed in the Community Building.

When I arrived back at Alexander, extraction was winding down as boats got out of the water for the night. The last high profile military vehicles brought the last group of evacuees to the extraction point. We cleaned up the area as best we could and prepared to leave.

As day three came to a close, we experienced our first example of the transition that would begin over the next few days, from the Private response to the disaster to the Government response to the disaster. Carly told me that halfway through the day, when things were at their busiest, FEMA (Federal Emergency Management Agency) came to Alexander. When they asked who was in charge, they were directed to her. They very curtly and directly informed her that they were taking half of the parking lot. After getting over her initial shock, she asked them what they expected her to do. She told them that clearly she was utilizing the whole parking lot for a system that was working to get citizens evacuated from flood waters and transported to friends or shelters. They restated their demand for half of the parking lot. When she proposed she shut down and "get out of their way," they informed her that they needed her to keep doing what she was doing. After further conversation, she conceded to their demands and mobilized her team to completely rework the system that was in place. FEMA proceeded to park one trailer on half of the parking lot and then sat and did nothing to help with the efforts. They

Leadership Lesson #10 - Leaders make good adjustments to changing circumstances. Leaders know how to make lemonade out of lemons.

never provided a reason for their demand. We, however, were too busy helping our neighbors to make a bigger deal of it. Our neighbors were in desperate need and we were committed to doing whatever it took to help them, even if it meant "changing on the fly" for the government.

This experience gives an inkling into the difference between private and government response in a disaster. Government employees who work in disaster relief do this type of work 24/7. They are

Leadership Lesson #11 - Leaders know that employees closest to the action and closest to the customer are the best people to make customer decisions. Leaders empower and cherish them.

around disaster regularly, seeing all kinds of human suffering on a routine basis. They work hard, but the vast majority cannot help but become desensitized to what is going on. This desensitization bleeds into how they interact with regular citizens who are serving out of passion and heart and just trying to help as best they can (help that is often accurate and well thought out).

Government employees can lose that personal touch for people who are impacted and must fight hard not to fall into that trap. For federal government responders, people in the disaster aren't their friends and neighbors. They aren't the people they see at the grocery store or at the gym. This is why, as much as possible, care during disasters should come from those in the community. We are the ones who are still sensitive to the impact. We are the ones who aren't just seeing faces, we are seeing our friends.

Ultimately, we estimate that the extraction point at Alexander that five "just trying to help how we can" folks launched that morning assisted close to 800 evacuees and saw a couple of thousand cars directed through the parking lot and into the flood zone to give assistance and supplies.

All day long, I had been getting texts from people we had helped get out of the water. As they were getting settled, they began thinking of the future and how they were going to rebuild. This was a foreshadow of things to come.

As usual, we spent the night networking and making plans for the next day. We had to coordinate with more people coming in to assist with rescue. The Fellowship had First Responders staying all over the building. The YMCA across the street opened for hot showers and logistics had to be worked out to make that happen. It was another long and fulfilling day.

Leadership Lesson #12- Leaders focus on organizing and empowering others to do the work. It is exciting and invigorating being in a boat rescuing people. Coordinating and organizing 10 boats to rescue people is the job of a leader.

WEDNESDAY

AUGUST 30 – An Active Shooter And Control Flooding

In a disaster, circumstances and information change very rapidly. This can cause a lot of frustration if you have never been in the middle of such a fluid situation. One moment, you are rocking along with a smooth operation helping evacuees, the next minute FEMA takes half the parking lot. One minute someone is telling you they are gonna ride the flood out, the next hour the water rises 5 inches and they are calling you begging you to get a boat to them and pick them up. One moment a boat crew is headed to pick you up, the next minute someone is floundering walking out of the flood waters and the crew has to attend to them.

On Tuesday, social media was a very effective tool for networking with those in the flooded waters. As we planned Tuesday night, our team felt that Wednesday would be much of the same, setting up extraction points and coordinating boats getting people out of the water. We drafted a Facebook post and shared it far and wide.

We had a team meeting on Wednesday morning and got the following pieces in place. We had a team of people ready to take calls and get the addresses out to boats. We had people ready to set up extraction points. We had shuttle drivers arranged to transport evacuees to the church for assistance once we got the extraction points set up. We were already coordinating rescues in various locations around West Houston and Katy with some of our boat contacts. We encouraged other boat crews to head east into Baytown and Galena Park, because we were receiving texts about significant needs there.

Jayson is a small group leader in our church. He had been landlocked until Tuesday and he and his wife were hosting a family from their group who had to evacuate. He is a member of the church and a good friend. Once the roads around his house were clear, he dove head first into helping on our team and played an integral role in what we implemented going forward. Wednesday, he and I were out at 5:30 AM evaluating the situation. We drove to the various extraction points we had worked out of on Tuesday and also ventured into the Highway 6 area to see how things looked (the maps on page one and two are helpful).

I set up shop in front of a big map in the foyer of the church. Before Harvey, the map was used to show people where our Small Groups

22

were located. Now, this map became an evolving picture of information we had about the flood. A picture that changed frequently.

Wednesday was a progressive revelation that those in our area who wanted to get out of their homes had gotten out. It seemed that the vast majority of people still in the flooded area in Katy had decided to ride things out. The rains had stopped, and they had electricity and some supplies. They could sleep upstairs in their own home and keep an eye on things (looting is always a fear during floods). Why risk leaving your home to sleep in a strange bed and worry from afar?

As it became more clear to us that people in our area were "hunkering down," we decided to expand the scope of our rescue activities beyond our immediate community. Many of the first responders who brought their boats had left family and jobs to come help. They didn't want to sit around and do nothing. They wanted to HELP people! I could definitely feel and identify with their frustration. The news continued to paint a grave picture, which it was, but in our area almost everyone, at this point, who wanted to get out of the flood waters had gotten out.

Things at the church were humming along with host homes being identified and matched with evacuees, donations being dropped off, and true support and help being given to evacuees (including lodging, food, supplies, and information). In our main building, volunteers were being registered. Evacuees were allowed to "shop" in our Worship Center for donated items that were being dropped off and sorted in our Children/Student building. We were also providing children/nursery care in that building for the volunteers serving on the campus.

Harvey was national news and The Fellowship was going above and beyond what most had ever seen. News agencies, always interested in the human story, were showing up. Pastor Jerry was juggling giving leadership to everything going on

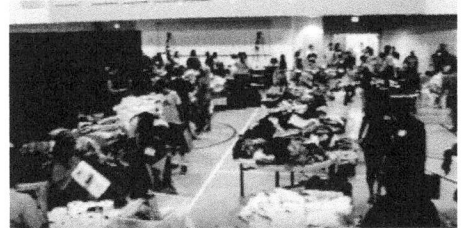

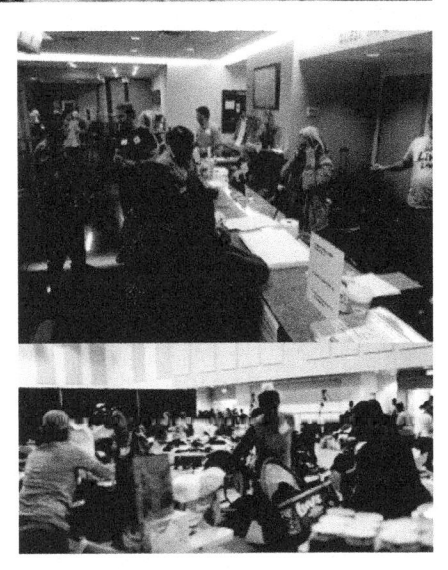

23

while also being available to everyone wanting to fathom how a church could mobilize to do so much in such a short amount of time. Our response to Harvey was a testimony to Jerry's dedication to our community and the Body of Christ in Katy. This was an effort not just of The Fellowship, but all the churches that he had networked with and ministered with throughout the last 20 years of his ministry at The Fellowship.

> **Leadership Lesson #13 - Leaders have a long-term dedication to their vision and give immense amounts of time, passion, and sacrifice towards that vision.**

While people in the flood zone in our area were somewhat in limbo, other areas near us were facing a grave situation. At this point in the catastrophe, the managers of the reservoirs were loudly proclaiming the integrity of the levies and their ability to protect greater Houston from further flooding. Those of us who are long time Houstonians knew this was not as much of a certainty as they were declaring. For the last 25 years, I had watched news stories or read articles every three or four years about the antiquated flood control system for Houston. These reporters usually concluded by discussing how it was important to spend the money to improve the reservoir system and the Addicks and Barker reservoirs themselves. That money never seemed to get spent!

One major concern was that The Interstate 10/Highway 6 area is the apex of the relief valve for both of the reservoirs. If the reservoirs became compromised or filled to capacity, water would be released into Buffalo Bayou. When the reservoirs were originally built, this area was sparsely populated. As with most world class cities today, Houston flows in one almost endless concrete jungle from Katy, along Interstate 10 on the far west side, to Baytown on the east side. The "relief valve" area for the protection of the reservoirs was now densely populated, and Harvey put the entirety of this flood control system to the test!

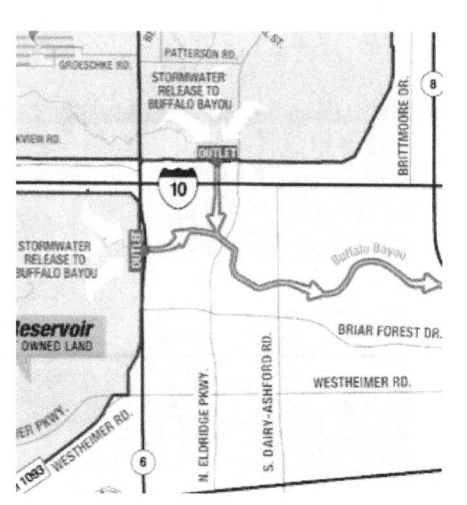

During Harvey, when the decision was made to release water from the reservoirs because they were in danger, the water flowed into the Buffalo Bayou, which caused it to overflow its banks and flood the Memorial area of West Houston (notice "Stormwater release to Buffalo Bayou" in both reservoirs on the map to the left). Sadly, both relief faucets for the reservoirs dump into Buffalo Bayou.

As designed by the flood control system, the Interstate 10/Highway 6 area were "control flooded" for the next several days to protect the levies. Both reservoirs were still filled to capacity and there was a cycle of releasing from the reservoirs into these areas, letting the water subside somewhat, then releasing more to flood the area and protect the reservoirs.

We began to transition our extraction team and shuttle services to this Memorial area. We were hearing people in these areas were in dire need. This area was also the most accessible area for our boats (it was on the far west side of the Houston flooding) and we had host homes waiting for evacuees that we could easily shuttle to the church. Jerry agreed that this was a good place to provide assistance and help to our extended community.

Once in this area, the team quickly realized that this was much more of a dangerous situation than our area. Along Interstate 10 (basically the southern boundary of the Addicks Reservoir) there were "bladders" (big, yards long balloons) put up to keep the Addicks Reservoir from flowing across the freeway. In the Memorial area, it was chaos. People trying to get out. Other people who had evacuated driving back in to check on their homes. Citizen First Responders trying to help. Government agencies trying to create some semblance of order.

It was made even more difficult as information changed by the moment. On top of this, water was rising in the area at various locations. In fact, there were rumors that the levee was significantly compromised and could give way at any moment. Rather than risking the team being stuck inside of the control flood zone, I encouraged them to get back west of Barker Cypress. As they got onto Interstate 10 they realized just how dire the situation was as water was beginning to flow over Interstate 10. They rallied with others we were working with, meeting at Texas Children's Hospital on the corner of Barker Cypress and Interstate 10 to consider where to set up an extraction point.

Once the location was identified, we could send other boats and High Profile Vehicles to the area to assist in the evacuation. We could also send trucks and Jeeps to help with shuttle service to the church. We were looking for a location that was accessible by boats on the flood side, but also accessible by vehicles from the dry side. Eventually, they decided to find an extraction point on Highway 6 somewhere near Interstate 10.

Standing at the map in the foyer of the Community Building, I was helping position our team and locate the extraction point. My help usually looked like texting, talking on the phone, consulting with others about what to do, and giving pretty specific directives to others on the team.

In the midst of this planning, the inconceivable happened. While standing at the door near the map, suddenly one of our amazing church members and Harvey volunteers came running across the courtyard from the Children/Student building, and burst through the glass doors screaming, "active shooter, active shooter!" I looked at her face and knew this was real.

The Fellowship sits on about 16 acres and we have two buildings at the southeast corner of Westheimer Parkway and Peek Road. These buildings are within 15 feet of each other and are connected by a simple walkway between them that forms somewhat of an open courtyard. The Community Building houses Kosmos coffee shop, church offices upstairs, and our double-sided basketball gym that also serves as our Worship Center on Sunday. At this point in time, there were approximately 200 people in the two buildings involved in various activities.

We quickly got the doors locked. There was one huge problem though. The Children/Student building across the courtyard, which she ran from into our building screaming "active shooter," was where we were providing childcare for our volunteers. Many of the parents of the children in danger in that building were volunteering in the building I was standing in. I distinctly remember the look of panic and agony in the eyes of one Mom as she realized that her children were in the other building where someone had just run from screaming, "active shooter, active shooter." The fear and anguish were heartbreaking!

Having been around disaster situations before, I had taken the precaution of carrying my pistol in my backpack —a backpack safely stored away in a room a few feet away! I knew I had to DO something, I couldn't just hang out there waiting to see what happened. I ran to the room and grabbed the pistol and ammunition. As an added precaution, I kept the gun unloaded (I wasn't

Leadership Lesson #14 - Leaders anticipate unforeseen problems AND make contingency plans and preparations for those problems.

thinking that was such a good decision at this point). As I opened the glass doors that led outside to the courtyard, I yelled to the people still outside, "anyone packing, anyone packing?" which is Texan for "is anyone else carrying a gun!?!" To my right about 25 feet away, a man was coming into the building through another door (there was a team of people cooking BBQ by the parking lot and he was one of them). He looked at me, gave a little nod, and rather than going into the building headed around the building to his left.

People had cleared out of the courtyard. There was a golf cart parked to the side of the entrance to the Children/Student building. I ran over to the cart and began shoving shells into the cylinder of my revolver. As I was doing this, two National Guardsmen at the corner of the building were taking turns poking their head around the corner to see if anyone was coming. As I got the gun loaded, I headed into the Children/Student building. I went down the hall to

27

the entrance that faces Westheimer Parkway where I could see people looking out the glass doors. Gunshots had been fired at the intersection of Peek and Westheimer Parkway, a few hundred feet away. The story that eventually came out was that it was a road rage incident. A man walked up to the car in front of him and started beating the driver through the window. The driver pulled a gun and shot his attacker through the car door.

One of the National Guardsmen from our community, who was assisting with our efforts at the church, helped get the situation under control. A nurse on duty at the church began treating the man who was shot. Police arrived quickly, despite the traffic, and set up a perimeter with "Do Not Cross" tape. We found out later that the attacker died at the hospital.

Before getting back to work, I had a conversation with officers at the scene. I specifically asked them to provide on site security at our church, given the number of volunteers and evacuees around the facility. Unfortunately, that never materialized so I spent the next few days whenever at the church, carrying my pistol. Even in Texas, it is highly unusual to see someone "open carrying," but then again, these were highly unusual times.

This was another example of a struggle the government has during times of unprecedented disasters. Government is staffed to keep the peace during normal times. When catastrophe hits, they are significantly understaffed for managing safety in the midst of the crisis. This is where the average citizen must step up to do uncommon things, things that normally would be handled by the government.

Despite as unusual a situation as an active shooter, everyone quickly got back to rescuing and assisting evacuees. Carly and the extraction team near Highway 6 heard about the shooting via texts as it was happening, but they had their own struggles. In this area, police were much more organized and controlling. Many streets into the flood area were blocked by barricades and officers. Fortunately, we were working hand in hand with the National Guard stationed at the church who were traveling with highly armed local officers. At this point in the efforts, they trumped

Leadership Lesson #15 - Leaders are humble enough to know there are important things they DON'T know. They network to find people with expertise that can help them get the job done.

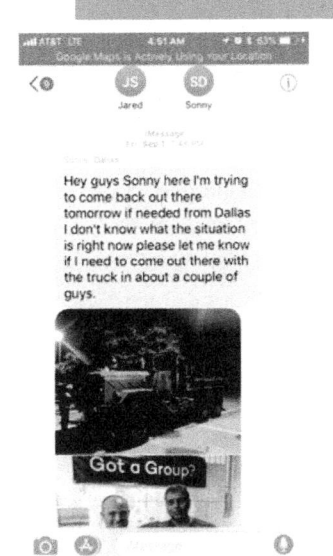

barricades and traffic controls every time.

Eventually, our extraction team settled in at an Exxon station at the intersection of Highway 6 and Memorial. This was right on the eastern edge of the Barker Reservoir levee and just outside the area being control flooded by the Addicks Reservoir. Rescue boats got into the water and the team helped evacuees as they could.

Throughout this disaster, I met and worked with some amazing citizens who put incredible amounts of time and energy into helping our community. One awesome contact was Sonny, a citizen First Responder from Dallas. Sonny came to Katy to help and was traveling with several boats and a High Profile Vehicle (HPV). HPV's are needed because specific boats run in specific depths of water. Sometimes, in floods, people must walk several hundred yards in knee deep water to get to a spot where a car or regular truck can drive. HPV's help transport evacuees to dry land. Sonny worked with us in this area.

On August 28th, he wrote, "We ran out of daylight and left 60 people in a school because it became too dangerous with water getting deeper, currents, and darkness. We DESPERATELY NEED A BIGGER BOAT, or several!!! All rescue efforts are by volunteers. Please help us save trapped people. We need a bigger boat by morning."

On August 29th, he told us, "Waters are rapidly rising. Tell anyone needing rescue to hang white towels from doors and windows, and to stay put until they see a rescue team." At this point, the Caveman Rescue Team were "wet, tired, and extremely grateful we were able to make a positive difference in the lives of so many families. The Team Volunteers are an amazing group of selfless individuals. I am so proud of them. Tomorrow morning we'll be back at it. Thanks to all of you for the emotional and financial support. Your support means the world to countless Texans, their friends and families, Caveman Rescue Team, and most especially, yours truly.

The next day, Caveman Rescue Team worked with several rescue teams, successfully getting over 500 people, and countless pets out of harm's way, south of Memorial Drive to Briar Forest, west from Highway 6, east to Wilcrest. The team in Port Arthur rescued and relocated numerous people, and four horses. Bruce displayed a picture on Facebook of a smiling dog. When asked about it, Bruce wrote, the (dog's) "owner is in LA on business. She left her dog, and cat with a neighbor; the neighbor apparently evacuated days ago, leaving the beautiful animals locked in an empty apartment. When she returns, her fur babies will be waiting."

Bruce was interviewed by Houston Public Radio, the National Public Radio's Morning Addition tomorrow morning, as well as Reuters News Agency. He also had a news crew from Italy riding along and accompanying them during their rescue efforts, and a news crew from Spain. They also took CNN Senior Medical Correspondent Elizabeth Cohen and her team of doctors and scientists out to get water samples to determine the pollutants, heavy metals, and chemicals in the floodwaters.

Bruce, my boat contact from McMeans the previous day, was working with a team of citizen First Responders that included several former Government First Responders. He headed for this area as well. We also coordinated other local boats into this area to help people get out of the water. Our extraction team worked with them through our extraction point at the Exxon station.

Another amazing contact was Terra. John and Carly met Terra at Alexander Elementary the day before, when it was an evacuation site. John, who is somewhat of a chocoholic, was so impressed when Terra brought them Snickers bars to snack on while they were working. I was introduced to Terra totally apart from Carly, through my boat contacts. I have Terra saved in my phone as "6 Boat Lady." When I first talked with her, she was helping direct six boats of citizen First Responders in the area making rescues.

Over the next few days, I got to know Terra well as she and her amazing kids helped in various ways. Terra and her husband were directly involved in relief efforts during Katrina, so she was a wealth of information and assistance. She was constantly on her phone listening to the chatter on Zello. Zello is an app that is a modern day CB radio. It basically turns your phone into a walkie talkie. You can listen to others on the system talking and when there is a break, take over the channel and talk as well. During Harvey, there were various channels set up (you have to sign in and it is administered). It is regulated because valid information is like pure gold and someone who was giving out bad info or dominating the channel with less urgent issues could be "shut down" by the administrator. Most of the citizen First Responders (like the Cajun Navy and many others) use this app. ZELLO was used during the day to direct rescues and coordinate efforts. It was used through the night to stage for the next day and facilitate lodging for those from out of town.

As the day ended, we had determined a few key adjustments. In our area, everyone who wanted out of the water was out of the water. Anyone still in the flood waters in their home, had decided to ride things out. This seemed like a reasonable decision given that the rain had ceased and the authorities were guaranteeing the integrity of the reservoirs (which were at capacity and then some). In fact, boats in the area around the church were now becoming shuttle services into the communities to help people check on their homes and take supplies to those still in their homes. This was something we determined we did NOT want to become, coordinators of boats running shuttle service into the flooded waters in our area. Rescue operations in the Memorial/Highway 6 area were still needed, although many people there were also

Leadership Lesson #16 - Leaders are comfortable clearly defining who they are and staying within that definition. They know that clarity of purpose and vision is vital. Leaders aren't afraid to say "no" to good things for the sake of great things.

riding things out at this point. One citizen First Responder jokingly said that people in apartments in the Memorial area had electricity, they had A/C for the heat, and they were just siting on their balcony watching the drama, drinking beer, and playing cards. At this point I began to wonder if there weren't some truth to his joke!

The work that was taking place at the church was an amazing service to the Katy community. As a leadership team our decision to use a host home strategy (church members and those in the community opened rooms in their homes to evacuees), rather than becoming an on site shelter, proved significant. Katy ISD was closing their shelters and encouraging people to take advantage of our host homes for lodging.

Not being an evacuee shelter made it possible for the church to become a hub for other key issues. We had become the "go to" location for evacuees! We served as a center for information and support. Evacuees were getting supplies, food, and vital information as FEMA and other government agencies, like the National Guard, worked closely with us to serve our community. We were also able to house government and citizen First Responders and provide them with a nice place to sleep, showers, and great food donated from a myriad of restaurants in the area.

Another shift in the disaster at this point was the freedom that regular citizens had during the disaster to "do whatever it took" to help and get things done. Over the last few days, when the hurricane initially hit, I had driven around police barricades, driven the wrong way on roads, driven faster than normal (I think you get the picture). I had been in a boat driving down a 4 lane road and "taken over" the parking lot of a school in the area to coordinate relief. I stood in a major street directing traffic for 30 minutes. These were highly unusual times!

As the urgency of the initial disaster was behind us, government agencies began to take back control. It was becoming more difficult for individual citizens to provide assistance as the Police and Sheriff's Departments, for the sake of order and the general welfare, began to take back responsibility for security.

This is part of the transition during a disaster. Initially, citizens respond however they can. Next, there is a season of cooperation between citizens and the government. And then, ultimately, the government takes over control of the response. We were definitely in the transition phase.

As night fell, our evacuation team got back to the church. We

Leadership Lesson #17 - Leaders make good decisions intuitively. They have a sense of what is the right thing to do in the moment. Often, it is a game changing decision.

> **Connie** ▮▮▮ with Carly ▮▮ nd 2 others.
> August 30, 2017
>
> Several times today...I sat in awe.....needing silence...helping...praying... sorting donations .....regrouping ...again in awe......we left our home several days ago believing and accepting it would be flooded when we returned...my husband was passionate that he didn't want to be stuck in home not able to get out and help others in need of rescue...as we left, the neighborhood flooded as one big river and no one could get in or out until today...so we were blessed to be at our daughters and son in law apt and all be able to help those less fortunate ...I am amazed at the way my husband, daughter and son in law stepped up , rolled up their sleeves and got in the trenches of Hurricane Harvey... as they worked from before dawn to late these past few days...we saw many lose everything and yet so grateful for rescue...my wonderful next door neighbor Maia ▮▮▮ was stuck at home alone with her young son, unable to get to her job as an ER Doctor, her husband Mark, an HPD officer was in Houston on duty...not only watched my home, sent pictures of water rising from the pond into our backyard, went in my home, checked on things, was able to get some food and rain boots and washed my dishes 😊 (now that's a awesome neighbor lol)...we've been in this home less than 5 months and have a neighborhood app and I have been immensely blessed to see this community become true neighbors in such a short time...everyone helping everyone , strangers became friends, Unity became essential...I am very grateful to be able to go home tomorrow with no flooding in my home....pure miracle... I am so proud of how this city came together and rescued, volunteered, donated, prayed, showed kindness, love, compassion....So thankful how our church opened doors for assistance, shelter, donations, tons of food, 200 host homes, and abundance of volunteers #caneislandrocks
> #lovemycity #thefellowship l#houstonstrong

coordinated getting first responders showers, food, and lodging. Everyone headed to wherever home was for the night to get some rest. Connie and I were able to get back into our neighborhood. We drove home to assess the damage and get settled back in. Fortunately, we hadn't gotten water in our home. I was definitely looking forward to sleeping in my own bed, and planned on getting a more reasonable start time at the church the next day. It seemed we were moving into a less frantic phase of disaster relief and might not even have many to help people evacuate on Thursday.

> **Carly** ▮▮▮ d a post — with Jerry Edmonson and 3 others.
> August 30, 2017
>
> [video - 837 Views]
>
> **Kristin** ▮▮▮ hecked in to 📍 Timewise Food Store with Carly ▮▮ nd 4 others
> August 30, 2017 · Houston
>
> We are setting up at the Exxon- we have boats and cars helping in Memorial plus blankets and food/ water. We will get you to The Fellowship so you can get matched with a home and hot meal and anything you may need. Water is rising quickly out here and first responders are kicking butt as well as locals to make sure people are pulled out!! US Army is here as well, Memorial/ Houston we got you!! #hurricaneharvey #relief #houstonstrong #memorialcity #prayfortexas #thefellowship

Fellowship Family,

The generosity of the community is overwhelming. If you haven't been up to The Fellowship, the church is packed full of supplies for the needs of those being evacuated. **Right now, please hold onto all your donations because we have no more room and because we will need them in the weeks to come.** I just sent this update out and thought I would share it with you.

> **The Fellowship is taking evacuees and matching them with host homes.** Yesterday we had an incredible outpouring from the community. We have had almost 300 families sign up to be host homes. We just opened up at noon yesterday and by 11 p.m. last night had over 400 volunteers sign up, 57 (169 individuals) evacuees made it to The Fellowship and 32 families were placed in host homes. We have experienced the generosity of God's people through an overwhelming response for supplies, food, meals, water, clothes, diapers, everything. We have so much and really don't need any more at the moment. If you have donations, hold onto them because we will need them in the weeks to come. If you can be a host home or help in any way you can go to this **link** and donate or sign up or just come by The Fellowship.
>
> **A big thank you to Greg Coop and the Monty Ballard YMCA.** Last night they opened their doors to 72 firefighters from Phoenix doing rescue operations. They have also opened the Y showers for all of our first responders, National Guard and citizen rescuers that we are housing here at The Fellowship. Greg was up here till after midnight working side by side with us to make sure we cared for those in need. Thank you.

Today is new day and we are expecting a new wave of evacuees to The Fellowship. Katy ISD shelters are full and are rerouting all new evacuees to The Fellowship for assistance. Thank you again for your prayers and all that you are doing to serve our city.

I am so proud of our church and difference it is making in the community. I am equally proud of the body of Christ in our city for the way that it is demonstrating the love of Christ. I am so looking forward to Sunday worship and celebrating all that God has done. I don't know what I'm going to preach, I may just get up and talk about all that God has done ... and weep.

Live Your Faith and Share Your Life

THURSDAY

August 31 - Mandatory Evacuation and Levee Concerns

During the night, things took a dramatic turn. Despite public communication from the Office of Emergency Management that the reservoirs were 100% reliable, at 1:00 AM the OEM sent a notification that we could expect imminent flooding in our area with record pool levels. At around the same time, the Fort Bend County Sheriff's office issued mandatory evacuation notices for people in the overflow areas of the reservoirs. The areas we had been working in!

This proclamation encompassed a significant number of homes in the Katy area. A mandatory evacuation means that government agencies can essentially force you to leave the area. This news was sent out as a community-wide notification and caused considerable concern throughout the community.

If you have observed any government response to a disaster, you know that there is often some aspect of competition between the various federal, state, county, and local agencies. We saw this expressed publicly and openly during Katrina in Louisiana between President Bush (a Republican) and Governor Blanco (a Democrat).

As our team evaluated the information, we felt that the OEM and Fort Bend Sheriff were expecting some fairly catastrophic event to impact water levels in our area. The rains had stopped and there was no other reason for waters to rise in our area other than from the reservoirs. The only event that could have "imminent flooding in our area with record pool levels" was a levee failure (similar to what happened in the New Orleans area during Katrina). Levee failure has a range of meanings, from significant water seepage under and around the dam, to large holes in the dam, to huge gaping breaks in the dam.

In our area, we were hearing that the devastation elevation was 104 feet. If your house was below 104 feet of elevation, you would be flooded; if it was above, you were outside of the flood zone (your house might be an island surrounded by water but it would not be flooded). Interestingly, Alexander Elementary, where we had set up extraction on Tuesday, was at 107 feet. It is noteworthy when you recall that FEMA took half the parking lot on Tuesday, for "no apparent reason."

The church was at a safe level at 105 feet. Basically the elevation slopes southeastward from 107 feet at Alexander and drops in elevation further south and east of Alexander where we had been rescuing our neighbors on Tuesday.

Making the evacuation mandatory, gave the Sheriff's office enforcement power. Throughout the day we got varying statements from the government as they backed away from this mandatory evacuation and sought to clarify their actions. At first it sounded like they were saying it was a miscalculation or a mistake. Other times it sounded like they were saying it was a misunderstanding on the part of citizens! I don't think we ever got clarity on what was going on.

We had a couple of people who began working the phones to find large shelters outside of our area (in Dallas, Austin, or San Antonio). This was a precautionary move in case of a legitimate mandatory evacuation for our area or even worse, a failure of the levee. If that really happened, there was no way those in our immediate area could provide lodging and care for everyone impacted.

From our perspective, it felt as if no one really knew how reliable the levees were. And when you think about it, how could anyone guarantee they would not fail, given that this flood was being called a 1,000 year event (something that had not happened for 1,000 years)? As such, we felt we should figure out for ourselves how to track the integrity of the levees . . . . somehow. After much conversation, we felt the best way was to insert people at various points coming south and west from the Barker levee. In our area, we were not as concerned about the Addicks Reservoir failing. If it failed, it would primarily flow south and east through the Memorial area along Buffalo Bayou. Overflow from an Addicks Reservoir failure would be identified by our plan, as well as a major failure of the Barker Reservoir.

To monitor this, we set our extraction at the very northern edge of the overflow for the Barker Reservoir (near Kingsland and Barker Cypress, just east of Baker Road). We would help people in this area as possible, as we also monitored the water levels. In addition, we had a young man who was driving in to join us from San Antonio with a jet ski. In the afternoon, he drove along Interstate 10 into the Memorial area giving us reconnaissance. He then put in the water at our extraction point closest to the levee and was monitoring water levels in that area with his jet ski.

Jayson was monitoring a little further south and west of there, at Pattison Elementary. This was a location Jayson and I were at the day before, so we had a point of reference for whether the water was rising or falling. We also placed people to monitor the water levels at the extraction points we had been at on Tuesday and Wednesday. There was no one evacuating from these areas, but if water began to rise it would be critical to initiate extraction points at those locations again. We felt that if there were a catastrophic failure, in our area it would be rapidly rising water rather than a wall of water. If the Addicks Reservoir failed, there were rumors that it would be a wall of water coming through that populated Memorial area pushing entire houses in front of it as it moved eastward. To visualize what this would be like, watch one of the many videos on YOUTUBE of people popping a hole in their above ground pools. Water can be a powerful force!

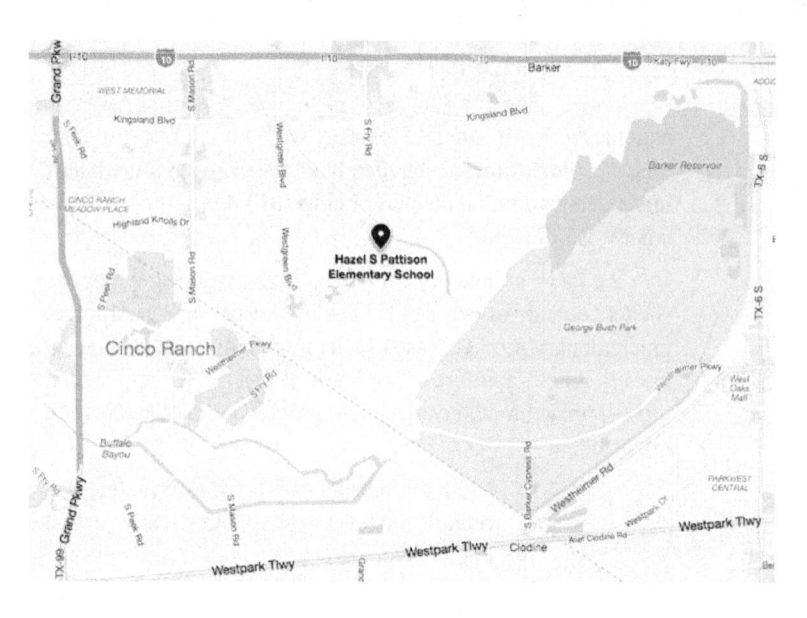

We spent most of the day helping as we could in various areas and working to get reliable information on the status of the levees. We coordinated some boats in the Memorial area as people were recognizing that flooding would continue for at least another week, as the powers that be "control-flooded" the area. One especially difficult situation was an elderly couple who were the parents of one of our staff members. Fortunately, we were able to successfully get them evacuated.

We were also hearing rumors that, at some point, electricity was going to

---

Leadership Lesson #18 - Leaders do whatever it takes to get accurate information. They know that without accurate information, accurate decisions can't be made!

be cut off to those in the flood zone. Until now, the only reason residents were able to stay in their homes was because they had electricity and A/C. If the electricity was turned off, the

> Kristin ▅▅▅▅ checked in to Chevron Houston with Carly ▅▅▅ and Kendy ▅▅▅
> August 31, 2017 · Houston
>
> We are set up here with first responders, boats, supplies, etc. If you know of anyone needing help out in Barker Cypress area or Kingsland please let us know! Water is too high for cars to get through but the boats are on their way to the homes and apartments in this area. The sun is out finally! Praise the Lord! #hurricaneharvey #relief #houstonstrong #prayfortexas
> One of the photos shows where we are putting the boats in, the other shows the area and intersection with roads closed!

heat would quickly "encourage" people to get out of their homes in these catastrophic flood zones. This was a legitimate option for the government in dire circumstances. We knew that, if this happened, we would have to reinitiate our rescue operations on a large scale. Our boat contacts were willing to hang around for a while in the midst of the uncertainty. Eventually they would need to get back to their normal lives or move on to areas closer to the gulf where active rescues were still taking place.

Another reason the boat rescue crews were willing to hang around was because there was further degrading of the situation to the west of us. The Brazos River was cresting over the next couple of days through our area. As it did, it was flooding areas west of us with "never seen" water levels. Some of the boat crews went to work there, in these newly flooded areas. ZELLO had a lot of chatter about boats staging to help with that possibility. These floods to the west of us were also related to Harvey. As Harvey moved north it dropped unprecedented amounts of water that flowed back south through our area to the coast, through rivers already at record levels.

At the church, adjustments were being made as well. The Worship Center was turned into an information resource center for FEMA and other organizations. It also housed a cafeteria for first responders and volunteers, as restaurants across the community continued to donate amazing meals. We were still housing many of the first responders at our facility and utilizing the YMCA across the street as well.

The Children/Student building was also used extensively. Downstairs we had storage for donated supplies, some housing for first responders, and childcare for volunteers. Upstairs we had set up a clothing/supplies store and a very organized system for walking those in need through the store to shop. Through the systems that were developed at the church, we provided much needed help to hundreds of our impacted neighbors.

We also continued to help evacuees by providing host homes. I remember talking with a gentlemen I knew from the YMCA. When he walked through the doors of the church, I went and gave him a hug and asked how we could help. He told me about his home being flooded, that he was living on a fixed income and needed a place to stay. We quickly set him up with a host home from our amazing database of Katy citizens opening their homes to evacuees. He was so incredibly appreciative of the help we gave him.

At this point, those who had not been directly impacted by the flood were in a transition back to "normal" life. It was an interesting dichotomy for a community. A significant number of our neighbors were drastically impacted by the flood. They were displaced from their homes and spending hours trying to figure out what the next step was for them. Their home was still flooded, but the waters were receding. They were looking at tens of thousands of dollars in repairs and trying to figure out what the government was going to help with and what insurance might help with. They were basically trying to figure out their next step to getting their life back to some level of "normal."

Others of us were simply inconvenienced by the flooding. Traffic was more horrific than usual. We lost a few days of work and lived through a headline, but essentially Harvey was just another dud of a hurricane for us, causing some disruption, but really not directly affecting us in a significant way.

In fact, by Thursday, jobs were calling most of us back to reality. John had to go back to work and others on the team were reintegrating into the grind of life. Fortunately, many of us chose to use any discretionary time we had to help our neighbors. As a church staff of about fifteen, we were working practically around the clock helping people. Most everyone else who attended The Fellowship was giving what time and energy they could to help. Katy ISD had graciously given teachers off until Wednesday, August 6. In fact, our Superintendent had proclaimed Friday, August 8 as a district wide "Help In The Community" day. Every school was to organize teachers and staff to be out in the community helping impacted co-workers and students. Students were returning to school on Monday, September 11.

Jayson and another long time friend who was a recent addition to the team, David, were in jobs with some flexibility to telecommute and work from home (and their offices on the westside of Houston were still in the

Leadership Lesson #19 - Leaders have a dedicated, cohesive team. They know that the sum is always greater than the parts. They know they are NOT the sum but a part.

flood zone). Carly was in a Master's of Social Work program through Baylor that was mostly online. Baylor was working with her on her schedule, and recognized that she was getting real life experience in her profession, as she worked in Harvey.

Another key struggle for those directly impacted by the flood at this time was finding good information. For many flood victims, they were in that transition phase from "the water is rising in my home and I have to get out" to "my house is flooded what are my options for getting back into my house and getting it fixed?" FEMA and Federal officials that respond to hurricanes were just now getting in place in our area (remember, there were many, many other Houston and coastal communities impacted by Harvey). Very few of us knew anything about the process for financing and physically getting a house from flooded to fixed.

Fortunately (not for them, but for the other hundreds of neighbors who had been impacted by Harvey), a couple of our staff members had been impacted by the Tax Day Flood a year earlier. Robert and Joe both had their homes flooded during 2016, so they knew much of the process for rebuilding, how to work with the government, what about insurance, things to watch out for with contractors, and hundreds of other questions. In fact, Joe's wife, Jessica, along with other concerned citizens, set up an amazing Facebook group called Hey Harvey. It was an awesome resource for people as they walked through the rescue to restoration process (and is still being used today).

Getting good information continued to be a struggle in the later stages of our rescue phase response to the disaster. I remember many times in the last few days that I had made it a point to get with the Sergeant and, at times, the Lieutenant, of the National Guard guys staying and working with us to give them a detailed update of what I knew. Not once did they give me any credible information. In fact, having worked around the government during crisis situations before, I wasn't surprised, but actually a bit amused, as they nodded and listened attentively, and then quickly got on the phone with their higher ups to discuss what I shared. I didn't hold it against these guys for doing what they were told. They are to be commended for following orders. I do, however, have a bit of a problem with the "higher ups" not giving them more freedom to share information with informed and highly motivated locals.

As the day wound down, I sat in the foyer of the church to grab a bite to eat and catch up with some of my team members. As I was finishing my meal, a young National Guard guy came and sat at the table by himself next to us, kind of eavesdropping on our conversation. I wasn't sure who he was and eventually introduced myself. He was the new Lieutenant taking over on a rotation for the unit assigned to us. I decided to download to him what I knew and asked him if he wanted to go for a ride around to see what was going on. He said he would like that. We jumped into Carly's Jeep and I took him to Alexander, the British Prep School, and McMeans to show him what was going on and share with him anything I knew about our situation.

We had an interesting experience on the way from British Prep to McMeans that would give a lot of insight into how we helped our neighbors during the restoration phase of our assistance. Driving past the light at Westheimer Parkway and Mason Road, a lady driving in a van began waving us down frantically. She was going our direction and headed towards the area by McMeans that was still flooded and impassable. She pulled alongside of us and we could tell she was distraught. I pulled into the left turn lane on Westheimer Parkway and she pulled behind me a few car lengths. We both parked our cars. I got out of the Jeep to go see what was going on. The Lieutenant didn't move, which seemed kind of odd (but I chalked it up to his training). As I walked back to her driver's side window, she began rolling the window back up and wouldn't talk to me! I'll admit, I looked a bit rough and may have still been packing a revolver, but it was definitely a surprise. After all, SHE flagged US down! I could see through the window that she was frantically trying to get someone on the phone and she was hysterical.

I walked back to the Jeep, and told the young Lieutenant what was going on. He got out of the car and marched to the window, which she was now rolling down . . . . for him. She was weeping and talking about going to work and trying to drive back home and the major streets were closed and she lived on Highway 6 and she couldn't get anyone at home on the phone. The Lieutenant commanded her to stop and commanded her to give him her phone. He shifted into full on "control mode" (which I understand is a part of his training). But in the process, he forgot . . . . her!

At this point, I jumped back into the conversation and said, "ma'am, how can we help you?" As she was crying, she said, "I just need to get back to the Grand Parkway, I don't know how to get to the Grand Parkway!" I said, "you just want directions to the Grand Parkway?" She said, "YES!" I told her, "do a u-turn right here and head back up Westheimer Parkway, in about 2 miles you will intersect with the Grand Parkway." She said, "really??" I said, "yes!"

Leadership Lesson #20 - Leaders know that every experience, good and bad, is a learning experience. It is a chance to gain information for improved decision making.

and she threw the van into DRIVE, drove around our Jeep, did a u-turn and headed back the direction she had come from.

After getting back to the church from showing the Lieutenant around, I tucked this experience in the back of my mind as a reminder of something very important. It was an amazing example that the government, despite the fact that it is made up of well-intentioned people, must fight against the tendency to lose its ability to truly show empathy and care for those they are helping. Structure and organizations are notorious for being cold and heartless. As we moved forward in our response as a church and community, we did not want to lose our heart for people. But how could we avoid that?

As the day came to an end, we were hearing that the government was still very concerned about the viability of the levees and getting our neighbors who were in the flood zone out of their homes. In fact, we had fairly credible rumors that there were plans to turn off the electricity to those areas the next day, which would effectively force our neighbors out of the flooding overflow area. We knew that if this happened, we would need to have extraction teams ready to help them get out of that area.

> Joey Beckham
> August 31, 2017
> We are coordinating with government agencies to help with extraction of people in the greater Katy area Friday at 6:00 AM. We will take people to a transition shelter where they can connect with friends or a host home we have in the area. If you need evacuation text one of these numbers: 817▪▪▪▪▪ OR 94▪▪▪▪▪4 OR 936-2▪▪▪▪▪

We again used social media to let people still in their flooded homes know that we were here to help. I worked with a few on the team to craft another Facebook post that could be shared far and wide, with phone numbers for people to contact. I put this up on Facebook late Thursday night.

In an attempt to get better information, I decided to go by the National Guard Command Center that was being housed in Katy High School on the way home. As I mentioned before, Katy ISD went above and beyond in opening our facilities to relief efforts. A huge warehouse center for the National Guard had been set up in north Katy. Around the school, helicopters were a regular sight (I listened to them from my bedroom window every night). If anyone had good information on whether we would need to run a rescue operation on Friday because they were shutting off the electricity to those areas, it would be someone from the National Guard Command Center. When I got there, the activity at Katy High School was impressive. Even at 10:00 PM things were humming along.

After sharing my story with a couple of different people, they had me sit and wait to see the Night Commander. While waiting, I had a nice conversation with an Army biologist who was in the area testing the flood waters. This conversation informed some of our decisions on Friday.

I eventually got in to see him. As with most organizations, they do things by the clock and I caught them on a shift change. This was another "aha" moment as we moved from our citizen response to our "working with the government" response. Government is around these types of disasters so much that they have systems and protocols. They have shift change that happens and aren't nearly as "grass roots" as we had been (with key leaders working and available around the clock). We ran more like the military in the midst of battle, they were running like a peacetime organization.

Despite approaching him from every angle I could think of to get him to give me SOMETHING . . . . ANYTHING . . . . about what was happening tomorrow, he wasn't forthcoming. While this was a bit frustrating, again, it was understandable. He had a boss who had a boss who all worked with others on a "need-to-know basis." I, as a regular citizen, was way down on that need to know list. I headed home with a couple of citizen First Responders we were hosting from out of town to get some sleep and prepare for whatever the next day held.

The flooding west of Katy in Simonton as the Brazos River crested.

FRIDAY

September 1 - Transition from Rescue to Restoration

We rallied at 5:45 AM at the map in the foyer to plan for the day. We continued to stage boats in various areas across west Houston and Katy. Even four days into the flooding, new people were still deciding to come out of the waters.

We spent a lot of time assisting citizen First Responders with boats to get in the water in other flood impacted locations. The Katy Mills Mall parking lot was a major staging area for boats throughout Harvey since it was at a very high elevation. ZELLO was rallying boats with government agencies to help out west as the Brazos was cresting. We had other teams from out of town who decided to head further east (traffic was clearing up so that it was no longer an all day drive). Others decided to go home to rest up and take care of family and business.

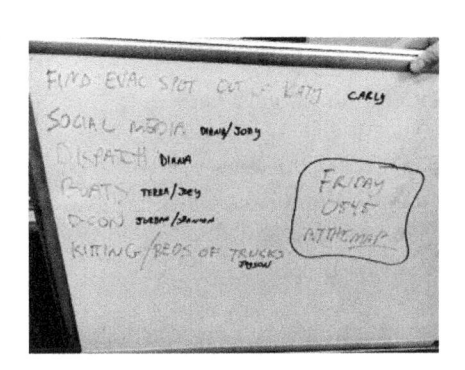

At this point, we were beginning to suspect that the threats to turn off electricity to the area were just that . . . . threats. It was very difficult trying to read between the lines of what the government was saying and what they did. Publicly, they were saying, "The levees are 100% reliable, we have absolute confidence in our system!" What they were doing sent a very different

Power being cut to homes under mandatory evacuation

A mandatory evacuation order has been issued for flooded homes south of I-10, north of Briarforest, east of reservoirs and west of Gessner.

KHOU.com, KHOU
7:39 AM CDT September 3, 2017
10:12 AM CDT September 3, 2017

Power is being cut off to approximately 300 inundated homes in West Houston that were flooded by the release of water from the Addicks and Barker-Cypress reservoirs.

A mandatory evacuation order has been issued for flooded homes south of I-10, north of Briarforest, east of reservoirs and west of Gessner. At 7a.m. Sunday, Centerpoint was to begin cutting off electricity to inundated homes in the zone. Electricity remains on for homes that weren't flooded.

message! Calling an emergency evacuation order at 1:00 AM in the morning. Giving warnings of "you better get out of the area because we are turning off the electricity." While shutting off the electricity did turn out to be just a threat in Katy, on Monday they actually used this tactic in Houston to get people to leave the Memorial area (the area that was being control flooded). While this is definitely an extreme measure, given the government's responsibility to insure safety, I believe it is within the scope of a reasonable response. It is often hard to protect people from their own bad decisions!

To monitor flood levels, we again staged people at locations where we had tracked flood levels the day before. Throughout the day, there wasn't much of a change and we juggled rotating people in and out of these locations. In fact, as the day progressed, the waters were receding in our area.

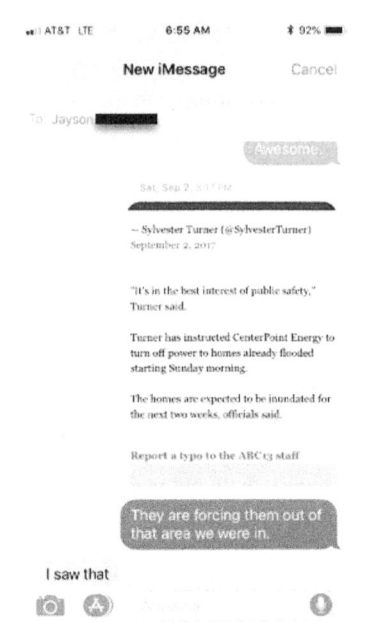

Another concern was that, by now, the flood waters had been sitting for several days in the hot sun. Sewage and chemicals had joined with the water to make an interesting mix of nastiness. The news was warning people about getting in the water and discussing the health hazards, especially if this water got into a wound. One major concern we had at this point was how to HAZMAT people coming out of the waters. How could we insure that they didn't walk out of the water with some flood related disease and spread it to responders and citizens?

What added to our concerns was that any new evacuee we transported would go to the church, a very public place. Food was being served all over the building and children were everywhere. We made the decision that anyone coming out of the flood waters into the facility would have to be DECONNED (decontaminated). We determined that this could be done simply by using hoses and lots of fresh water and detergent. An even better option was a cleaning station that various government agencies traveled with (basically a portable shower with lots of detergent available).

I distinctly remember one conversation with a government agency. We had been partnering together to rescue people and I told them that, at this point, we wanted them to take responsibility for DECON of people who came into contact with the flood waters. We would gladly transport them to the church, but only after they had been rinsed off. This agency had a wash station they set up nearby to help with this important new development.

In every disaster, there is a distinct moment when citizen First Responders realize that it is time to transition their emergency response efforts to government agencies. We realized it was time for the government to take over what we had been doing to rescue people. Friday was the day our rescue phase ended. One key issue was this contamination concern.

Security concerns were another big reason to transition rescue to the

Leadership Lesson #21 - Leaders know when it is time to redeploy assets from less effective or duplicative efforts to other areas. They know when to hold 'em and when to fold 'em!

government. Looting was beginning to take place in the area. In the afternoon, we got word that there were looters in the neighborhood who had been identified and chased out of a house. We were warned that they might be lurking in the woods near the church. The National Guardsmen, who were on site, went and searched around a bit, but didn't find anyone.

At this point, most of the citizen First Responders in our area were going out into the water with police escorts or National Guardsmen. We had built such a good relationship with the National Guardsmen at our church that we worked seamlessly together.

We also had a couple of cars broken into at the church. When security issues become routine, that is a good indication that you are entering a new season where rescue is primarily coordinated by the government.

Another reason we knew it was time to transition rescue operations to the government was the reality that, in our community, things were shifting from a rescue mode to a restoration mode. We had gone a couple of days with little or no rain. Major flooding from rains in North Texas was occurring west or east of us, but really not impacting our community directly at this point.

In fact, the waters were beginning to recede in our area. Many evacuees were finding ways to drive or walk into their neighborhoods to evaluate their homes. When they got there, they discovered they had a long road of clean up and recovery ahead of them and they began asking us to help them. Several church members and neighbors became "test cases" for the hundreds we would help going forward.

We also had relationships with people from out of town who wanted to send supplies to our community. At this point, we did not need water, clothes, or food items anymore, we needed tools and resources to help people clean up and rebuild.

At the church, things continued to hum along like clockwork. Staff and volunteers had organized an amazing response to the crisis. First Responders and volunteers were being worked, fed, and housed. Evacuees were still coming to the church for necessary supplies, resources, encouragement, and information.

We continued to run a store out of the Children/Student building. Evacuees and those needing supplies were seated in the Loft Worship where they were loved on and given food and water. As their name was called, they were allowed to go into our Loft Commons where they shopped for needed clothes and supplies. I remember being pleasantly surprised to walk in and see a teaching partner from McMeans, with a microphone in hand, announcing the names for shopping. It was truly amazing to see the church and the community working hand in hand. Even now, it brings tears to my eyes thinking about it.

There were a few interesting challenges that developed given that we were giving away vast amounts of "stuff" to individuals. We had determined that we were very willing to help anyone at least once, but we would work hard not to be scammed by anyone. We know there is a difference between helping and being used.

I remember one family that day that I helped shop in the store. One key shopping requirement we had was that families provide an address in greater Katy. A family came for help who did not have any local info or address. However, they had some type of local identification and a good story, so I got them some food to eat and walked them through the store getting what they needed. We had conversations about their family dynamics as we shopped.

When we got outside, I noticed that they had Maine license plates on their car. I asked them nicely about it and they said they had recently moved down. They asked about getting more supplies and mentioned that they had significant ongoing needs. I encouraged them to make their way to one of the major shelters in Houston where they were set up with FEMA onsite, extensive supplies, and ongoing resources. It felt like they were looking to get in on some of the money that FEMA might be giving to those impacted down the road.

Another family had shopped through the store several times and I was tasked with asking them to find someplace else to get supplies. It was a bit awkward asking them to leave, but we felt that we needed to be good stewards of what had been donated and that meant insuring that these donations were used wisely.

The Red Cross showed up at the church in the afternoon in a metro bus. They were driving through the area distributing various supplies that they had identified as necessities for the future clean up operations in the neighborhoods (bleach, plastic tarps, brooms, shovels, and other items in an Emergency Bucket). They "randomly" stopped at the church looking for a restroom. We gathered volunteers and began unloading everything they would give us. We definitely had contacts with a lot of neighbors who were going to need clean up!

As things wound down at the church, I made one last round to make sure things were secured. As I got to the back door, a car pulled up to the locked doors. It was a family of four in a nice Sedan. The Dad got out and I went to talk with him. He said he and his family had gotten out of their home very quickly in the rising waters and he just needed some shoes for his son. I asked him what he did and where he lived. He mentioned a subdivision in our area and that he was a manager for an assisted living facility nearby. The joy they had as they shopped through the items in our store was fulfilling. The celebration we had when they found a pair of shoes for his eight-year-old son was inspirational!

At the end of the day, we were asked to help set up boats for a government organized delivery of goods to a landlocked community south of us. Most of the citizen First Responders in our area were moving on to other locations or going home. Despite the fact that we were winding down our rescue operations, Terra and I spent long hours working the phones to set up this operation. We coordinated with the ZELLO administrator to have boats ready. I also worked with a boat contact we had in the area to go out the next morning to evaluate exactly what kind of boats we needed.

The last thing we wanted to do was send another boat crew on a wild goose chase. At this point, Terra, was hearing on ZELLO that citizen First Responders were feeling a bit used by the government as they were staged here to do nothing, then staged there to sit around and do nothing, then moved down south to hurry up and wait. Their service to our community was too precious to us to do that to them, so we worked hard to make sure we had good information on the mission for Saturday.

Leadership Lesson #22 - Leaders know that others' confidence in them erodes if they over promise and under deliver. Their integrity depends on delivering what they promise!

47

SATURDAY
September 2 - What If?

At 6:45 AM, we began coordinating boats for the local government agency to assist the landlocked community south of us. Our immediate area was moving into the restoration phase. We didn't need to organize rescue in our area because the few people who needed rescue were getting help directly from the government.

We also decided not to provide any more evacuations or organize boat rescues further east of us because of contaminated water issues. In the Memorial area, they were saying that a waste water treatment facility had been impacted and significant amounts of sewage water were being mixed with the already "ripe" flood waters. We felt, at this point, the government should be able to handle needs in that area as they continued their controlled flooding to manage water levels in the still full reservoirs.

Terra and I worked with ZELLO and our local contact to get things ready for the delivery south of us. At 8:00 AM, we received the message that the delivery mission had been aborted, but there was another need at another location. At this point, Terra and I decided we should get out of the middle of setting up government rescues, that may or may not happen, and let the government work directly with boat contacts for these "might happen" needs.

This is another example of the difference between government response and citizen response. At this point in the crisis, it felt like government agencies were transitioning into "we are gonna be at this a while" mode. It was becoming "job like" for them with shift changes and a "we gotta pace ourself" attitude.

This isn't necessarily a bad thing! Our government responders work very hard, they have a life outside of their job and must develop a pace and rhythm to survive. This is not the case for citizen First Responders. Many of us were taking time AWAY from our jobs to be here helping. Government employees were coming into it as a PART of their job. We were giving time to this that was time we were taking from our families and our jobs. As such, citizen First Responders have little patience for "hurry up and wait" and missions that seem to change on a whim (maybe it wasn't really a whim, but it was beginning to feel that way).

This transition from citizen First Responders to government control of the disaster response was actually a good thing. It meant that the catastrophe was transitioning from an emergency situation to a recovery situation. From truly life or death, where normal citizens did abnormal things, to a more paced response. We were moving from the rescue phase to the restoration phase.

Our neighbors were no longer frantically concerned about getting out of their homes because of rising floodwater. They were concerned about how to recover and restore their homes. Our neighbors were beginning the long road back to normalcy, a road that many would be on for six to nine months (in fact, some would still be on it a year later).

Over the last week our team had been involved in helping hundreds of people in a life-threatening emergency. We had worked with thousands of people organizing emergency response to a very fluid situation.

Doing this felt good. It felt good to help our community!

It also felt good that this type of help wasn't needed any longer!

What was next for our team though? Clearly, recovery from this event for our neighbors was going to be an ongoing process of months, not just weeks. What role might we play in that process? Are there things we could do to help? Should we play a role?

At the church, amazing teams had been developed around various staff members to carry out the services that were being provided. I did not feel that getting our team connected into one of those teams would be the most effective use of our skills. In fact, most of the teams and systems that had developed were going to "fade away" in the next few days, just as the need for our rescue and recovery system faded away. Our impacted neighbors were going to begin to focus their energies on rebuilding, not survival.

One major issue that we had discussed as a staff throughout the week was how we could be involved with our neighbors for the long haul. How would we walk with them as they began to navigate the daunting task of restoring their homes?

In this conversation, Pastor Jerry had asked what it would look like for there to be a storage facility for the vast amount of resources that people would give to help in the recovery. What if there were eventually a warehouse where our impacted neighbors could pick up donated sheetrock, tools, carpet, tile, and even furniture to replace what was lost? What if we leveraged the good will of people across Texas and the USA who wanted to give towards recovery by having a centralized area for them to donate tangible items?

As a team, we talked about whether we could help put feet to this idea. How could we make this idea a reality? We knew that resources were going to begin flowing into our community. When a disaster like this happens, people in the United States will respond generously.

We were already talking with a gentleman who wanted to donate a semi-truck load of sheetrock. We knew he had the means to make this a reality. The problem is, sheetrock wasn't needed . . . . yet. Vast amounts of it would be needed within three or four weeks, though!

We decided to take on the task of finding warehouse space and working on the next phase of operation, the restoration phase. We talked with Jerry

> **Leadership Lesson #23 - Leaders anticipate future needs and address those needs proactively. They try to be ahead of the curve!**

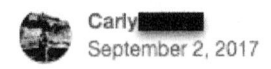

Carly
September 2, 2017

PLEASE SHARE:
Our current need with The Fellowship is an empty warehouse/retail center/store that we could use as a distribution center. Do you have any information or connections with a property like that in the Greater Katy area?

Right now in Katy we are trying to transition to long term recovery (for our immediate area and beyond). Our church, The Fellowship, has paired over 80 displaced families with host homes. We currently have an additional 300 host homes available for first responders & Katy area evacuees. We have been running a store where over 550 families have "shopped" for clothes, food, everyday items, etc. We have a "pharmacy" that has been filling prescriptions. We are stocked with donations and are still receiving semi trucks full of supplies from all over.

about it and he said, "go for it!" He simply asked that we work with Glenn, our Missions Pastor in the process. Glenn would ultimately be giving leadership to our response.

Jayson, David, Carly, John, and I began brainstorming how to find large amounts of warehouse space. We decided that, once again, social media was a good vehicle to communicate the need and the vision. We also literally began driving around town and calling realtor numbers on properties that were vacant that might fit our needs. We chased a lot of dead end leads, but towards the end of the day had a couple of promising ones.

As we worked to find warehouse space, we also began interacting with staff members and others who were looking towards clean up. Over the last couple of days, while we were running the rescue operations, we connected with various neighbors who were able to get to their homes and evaluate the situation and consider their next step.

Thankfully, the flood waters had receded in our area, but anything that sat in water in the heat for a couple of days was already growing mold. Furniture, cars, things in the garage, doors, baseboard, sheetrock, insulation, carpet, and hardwood floors all would have to be trashed if they sat in water. Even six inches of water for more than a day or so in the heat was devastating. This happened to 14,000 homes in our area!

We knew that the next step for everyone impacted would be clean up (sometimes called "demo" or "muck out"). In fact, we had been networking with various church members and people from out of town who were beginning to demo homes already.

The problem was, where would we find the expertise to demo homes? We knew this was the next big issue. If every company in Houston that knew how to do mold remediation got to work 24/7 there would still be thousands and thousands of homes sitting for days waiting for help.

At this point, the greatest enemy we had wasn't flood waters; it was mold. As one Pastor said, "mold doesn't wait!" Left to its own, without a quick response, mold will grow in a house, within a week or so, to the ceiling!

Fortunately, a long time friend of mine was leading his church's efforts in Pasadena and they were already demoing homes. In that area, the waters had receded much more quickly than our area, where we were overflow for the reservoirs. I began reaching out to Pastor Billy to see what they knew. We also had church members who were already demoing their home with the help of loving church members who knew what they were doing, people that had a background in construction.

Up until this time, our team had been a very loosely organized network of grass roots people responding to a rapidly changing emergency situation. We had to nimbly adapt and improvise on the fly. Our network became very broad, but it was very relational, unstructured, and fluid.

As we looked toward the future of the response, we knew it was important to develop a clear vision and strategy. There would need to be a sustainable response to the crisis. As such, we put time and thought into the structure as we were flowing along tying up loose ends from the rescue phase, hunting warehouse space (something we knew we needed), helping people where we could, and juggling our own personal responsibilities.

Jayson and David, with their business management experience, were a wealth of help and information in this vision casting process. We began with the vision and brainstormed around what we felt we could do and what we felt God was calling us to do. As a church, we always taught that we are to be the hands and feet of Christ as we are telling others the Good News. It seemed this was a great opportunity to show up for that passion.

We also knew that this was going to be a huge task. We weren't just talking about a few dozen homes flooded by Harvey. There were thousands upon thousands of homes in the greater Katy area who would be rebuilding for the next several months.

As we brainstormed, we identified key questions and issues we would need to address. How would we gain the expertise to demo houses on a large scale? What structures would need to be in place to store and distribute resources? How would our impacted neighbors avail themselves of the supplies we had on hand? How would we move stuff from one place to another? Is it really feasible to help people rebuild their homes after they are demoed? What would an organization like this look like? Who would we need to onboard to help with this? Could we really do this with volunteers? Could we do this and continue being the church and not a relief agency? How do we avoid the tendency of agencies to rescue people rather than partner with them in their own recovery? How could we maintain "high touch" with those impacted as we developed an organization? Could we really "get the job done," while being sensitive and caring towards the individual impacted?

At the church, we were consolidating resources out of the Worship Center (Sunday comes around every week and tomorrow was Sunday). Friday night, an amazing crew of volunteers moved everything from the Worship Center to the Children/Student building. Everything we had been doing to provide supplies to flood victims was now housed in the Children/Student building, including donations that had been piled up outside the building. We planned on continuing to function as a resource center for flood victims and the Children/Student building would primarily be used for that (as well as temporary housing for First Responders and demo teams).

Joey Beckham
September 3, 2017

If I get too philosophical in this post please forgive me. It has been a long week with 15 hour days. One thing I'm learning from Hurricane Harvey as I helped develop a shelter for 600 people and helped evacuate 1000 people from the neighborhood behind my church, as I looked at the pictures of the house of a good friend with 10 inch water mark lines on the inside wall and listened to the plea of the government when as a last resort to get people out to safety they turned their electricity off in the Memorial area in Houston: GOD IS LOVE! Somehow, someway. Let me explain it like this : "Jesus loves me THIS I KNOW, for the Bible tells me so, little ones to HIM belong, they are weak but he is strong. YES Jesus loves me, Yes, Jesus loves me." No. Matter. What! My circumstances will never change that. And here is the good news for you . . . He loves YOU to! Please pray for the greater Katy, Texas area. We are 300,000 people working together to recover from this devastation.

During our services on Sunday in the Worship Center, FEMA would use our Community Room to meet with impacted neighbors throughout the day. Sunday was definitely going to be an unusual day at The Fellowship!

SUNDAY

September 3 - The Water Came Up And The Walls Came Down

Sunday morning, Jayson, Carly, John, and I met at 8:45 AM to discuss the restoration vision. Often clarity develops after sleep and time. One key thing that God had been speaking to me was, "how big is your faith, do you believe I can do this?" I was asking myself and asked the team, what would be a God size vision?

As we talked and prayed, we felt we should see where this could go. We knew it would take a team to pull this off, so we articulated a vision and identified mission critical items to get it done. We scheduled a meeting for 4:00 PM and began inviting people we felt might resonate with what we were planning.

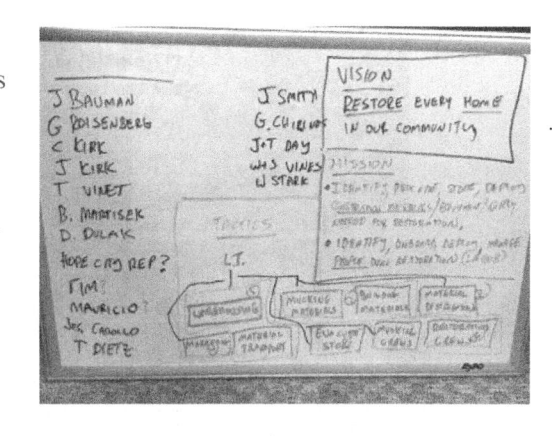

The service Sunday morning was an awesome celebration of God and His presence in the midst of hard times! It was especially amazing to have the National Guard participating. One of the guys even played in the band in his uniform!

Pastor Jerry had an awesome message of hope, encouragement, and counsel. He began with a wonderful statement of reality for our community, "When the water came up, the walls came down!" This was something all of us had experienced that week, as we watched a community come together to fight a common enemy. People were shaken out of their comfort zone by the circumstances of life, shaken to a point where we had to depend on one another! Jerry shared some of the amazing things that had been accomplished in our community.

He ended the message with a wonderful challenge to grieve well. Grief is a response to loss, and we had definitely experienced loss. He challenged us to do the hard work of walking through the grieving process and moving from the "bitter" side of shock, anger, and resentment to the "better" side of acceptance and hope. We ended with a

SARAH Curve
Shock Anger Resentment Acceptance Hope

53

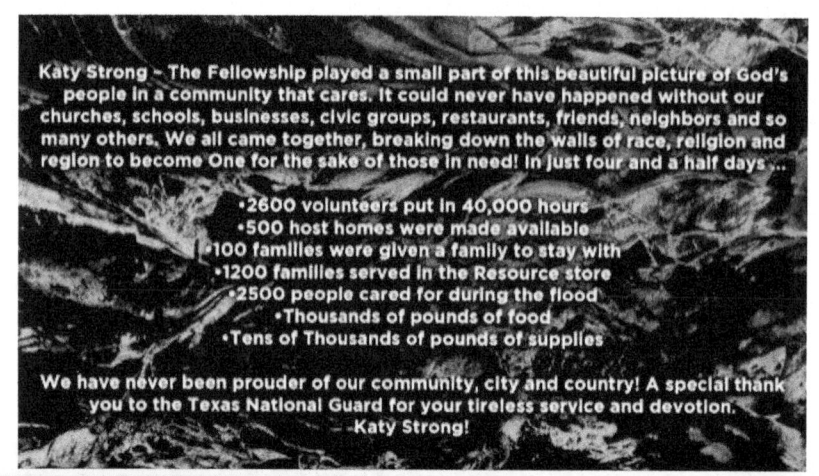

> Katy Strong - The Fellowship played a small part of this beautiful picture of God's people in a community that cares. It could never have happened without our churches, schools, businesses, civic groups, restaurants, friends, neighbors and so many others. We all came together, breaking down the walls of race, religion and region to become One for the sake of those in need! In just four and a half days ...
>
> - 2600 volunteers put in 40,000 hours
> - 500 host homes were made available
> - 100 families were given a family to stay with
> - 1200 families served in the Resource store
> - 2500 people cared for during the flood
> - Thousands of pounds of food
> - Tens of Thousands of pounds of supplies
>
> We have never been prouder of our community, city and country! A special thank you to the Texas National Guard for your tireless service and devotion.
> —Katy Strong!

wonderful time of prayer for those impacted.

Between services, I had a chance encounter (more like a God encounter) with the husband of one of our staff members who was flooded. I had been involved in helping them over the last few days. He was very concerned about the future and how this was already impacting them, straining their family dynamics with all the added stress. I encouraged him and told him that we were committed to being the Body of Christ, the hands and feet and heart of Christ for his family. I resolved at that moment to be their advocate through the process of getting help from the church. I resolved to "own" insuring that they got restored.

This experience weighed on me throughout the next couple of days as we were brainstorming how we would respond during the restoration phase of

Leadership Lesson #24- Leaders know the importance of self care and help those that work with them avoid burnout. They actually care about the people who work with them.

this tragedy. Would we become just another cold, heartless organization that became a "black hole" for people needing help or would we find a way to treat people as human beings, not as a victim or an inconvenience?

Since Harvey began, I had been networking with Pastor Billy, my old friend at Antioch Houston, who was already running hard in the demo phase. In fact, by Saturday they had demoed over 50 homes! His Facebook page is an amazing timeline of their response, as people from their network of churches and others from all over the USA drove into Houston and went to work!

As I talked with Billy, I realized we needed to get a crew over to Pasadena to learn from what they were doing. A church member had some friends in town from Georgia to help demo houses. I had been networking with them on Saturday and I asked Todd and Phillip if they would be willing to go over and learn from Billy and their organization on Sunday afternoon. Todd said they would go wherever they were needed the most. They spent the rest of the day with Billy and were a huge help in our learning curve on how to demo a house and systems we needed to put in place to run crews.

We met at 4:00 PM in the Loft Commons with potential team members for our

---

Billy Sieh
August 31, 2017 · Twitter

We already have over 400 relief workers headed to Houston. @AntiochWaco & @AntiochCS already in homes helping. #antiochmovement @AntiochHOU

Billy Sieh
September 1, 2017

If you live in the Houston area and want to help, but don't know how to: COME TO OUR OFFICE TODAY WITH A GROUP AND WE'LL PUT YOU TO WORK. 1635 Broadway St., Pearland, Tx 77581 Preferrably with a team of 10-15 people.

Billy Sieh
September 2, 2017 · Twitter

Our volunteers removed every bit of moisture (sheet rock, flooring, furniture, insulation, etc.) from 25 houses yesterday. @AntiochHOU #wow

---

Billy Sieh
September 2, 2017

Just heard a story about a professional moisture removal crew walking down the street signing people up to have sheet rock, flooring, and everything else wet removed for $7,000 in 7-10 days. Our crews walked up, heard, and offered to do it for free right then. Woman cries. House is taken care of. COME HELP! Mold will grow if we don't remove the moisture. #loveyourneighbor #helphelphelp

---

Billy Sieh
September 2, 2017

We sent out a 200-300 more workers...adding to the 100-200 that are already out. If you want to help and don't know what to do: COME! If you have a home that needs water extraction and sheet rock/flooring/furniture removal: COME! Let the Church be the Church. Forget denominations, banners, titles, COME! Let's love our neighbors. 1635 Broadway St., Pearland, Tx 77581. We will train you and send you out. We will put your address on the list and get to it ASAP. We have several hundred more volunteers coming in and we're knocking out 25+ houses a day in great detail.

Billy Sieh
September 3, 2017 · Twitter

By the grace of God we have been able to remove all wetness from 82 homes. The more workers we have, the more homes we can save. @AntiochHOU

> **Something really special is happening in our neck of the woods.** @AntiochHOU
> #antiochmovement

> **Billy Sieh**
> September 3, 2017 · iOS
>
> You don't need to know what you're doing. We will train you and put you with people that do. Please come!! 1635 Broadway St., Pearland, Tx 77581

> **Billy Sieh**
> September 4, 2017
>
> My house is behind this pile of trash. Just finished 30k worth of work on this fixer upper in August. Thankfully the appliances are undamaged and my guys living there didn't lose much.

> **Billy Sieh**
> September 4, 2017
>
> Hey friends. I think the damage to our rental house (7 guys from church live there) is finally sinking in. There's been so much adrenaline these last few days helping so many other homes that I haven't had much space to think about it and now that I'm seeing pictures of the demolition and thinking through replacement and rebuilding costs...it's finally hitting home. Also....on hold with FEMA for a wait time of 111 minutes...They have been telling me 111 minutes for the past 20 minutes. Something went wrong with my online application, which was confusing. I don't know what I'm gonna do...I can't imagine how many other people feel this way. PRAY FOR OUR CITY AND THE COUNTLESS PEOPLE WHO ARE ASKING THIS QUESTION. I don't know where I'd be without the church. Thank You Jesus!!! Thank you Church!!

> **Billy Sieh**
> September 17, 2017 · Twitter
>
> 220+ homes mucked out in the last 2ish weeks! Churches from CA, CO, LA, NB, AZ, and all over TX have come to love & serve Houston. #thankful

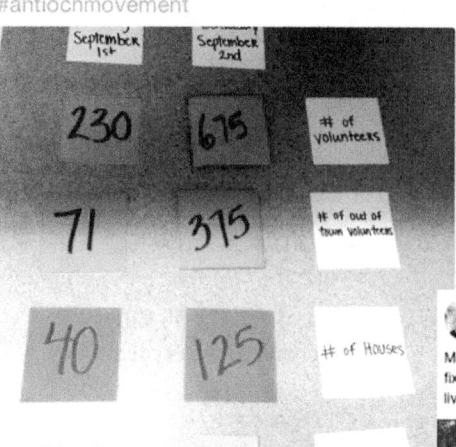

restoration plans going forward. We had identified several mission critical elements that would need leadership from high capacity individuals. Roles included coordinating out-of-town teams that would be coming to serve our community, social media/advertising, warehouse coordinator, demo team coordinator, and care coordinator (someone to manage a team that would insure that we remained a "high touch" organization for our impacted neighbors). This meeting was not a hard sell to get people involved, but an opportunity for people to step up and continue serving our community. We knew that we didn't want people serving out of compulsion, but out of a sense of Godly call and leadership. We had several people commit to help beyond our current team.

Throughout the day, churches that had been impacted were making use of our facility on Sunday for their Sunday service. Yes, you read that right, churches were actually working together to the extent that they were sharing facilities for Sunday services! In fact, a local Church of Christ used our facility every Sunday for several months after Hurricane Harvey as their building was being repaired.

Before heading home, I swung by to update Glenn on our progress (he was staying with friends in the area). Glenn had his own personal Harvey experience. Glenn lived on site with his wife at a women's facility our church had recently developed in far north Katy. His area had flooded badly and Glenn was not able to get out of his house until late on Tuesday. As the Missions Pastor, he already juggled a lot of balls and all of those were suspended in the air as he was getting up to speed on leading our Harvey response.

Going forward, staff members who had been doing a lot around Harvey planned to offload their Harvey responsibilities to him. At the same time, he and I were working on our ongoing response to the disaster as we transitioned out of emergency mode. In our relationship, Glenn was working a lot of organizational angles in our transition as I worked on a system that would serve us going forward. We reviewed what the team had developed organizationally and discussed transitioning out of providing clothes and supplies to those impacted. Other churches were planning on continuing store operations. Discontinuing our store sometime this week, would free us to focus on the demo phase. We set up an 8:00 AM meeting with Jerry to keep him in the loop on the plans.

Leadership Lesson #25 - Leaders work hard to communicate well both ways on the chain of command. Down to those under them and also up to those above them.

MONDAY

September 4 - Mold Doesn't Wait

On the way into the church Monday morning, I was amazed to see homes near my house that already had piles of trash in front of them. The streets of North Katy had dried out much more quickly than the neighborhoods in the reservoir overflow areas. In south Katy, piles of cabinets, furniture, and sheetrock in front yards would be a familiar scene for the next several weeks. I was also encouraged by the beautiful sunrise marking a new day, a new beginning!

At this point in our Harvey experience, we were wrestling with a seismic shift of focus. Until now, we as a church and a community had been focused with laser precision on one thing: how do we respond to this "life or death" crisis of a flood? What am I going to do RIGHT NOW to help myself or my neighbors in this catastrophe? We had run rescue operations for people needing to come out of flood waters and we had provided manpower, resources, lodging, and information to our affected neighbors.

A week into the event, however, things had significantly changed. Families who had fled to other cities to ride out the flood were back in town. Jobs were calling us back (I was expected to report to my school on Wednesday). In fact, for many who were not directly flooded, the greatest inconvenience during the second week after the event was worse traffic than normal due to major road closures. And that problem was gone within another week or so!

No longer were people wrestling out of their flooded homes carrying what they could grab in a sack, wading through thigh deep flooded waters looking for shelter. Now they were looking to get back into their home, to begin the road to restoration.

For those who did not get water in their home, who were only displaced by flood waters, this was a fairly quick transition. For those who got water in their home, they were looking at several weeks, months, or even a year or more.

Helping Organizations were in a transition as well. There is always the hope that government will come in like a Super Hero and save the day. Those of us who had been around these events before knew that wasn't the case. The government is a very slow moving organization, that promises a lot, but rarely delivers to the extent of their promise. And more often than not, if they do

Leadership Lesson #26 - Leaders fight hard against the tendencies of organizations to become self focused rather than customer focused.

deliver, it is going be be after a lot of paperwork and vast amounts of time.

This is the reality of large, complex organizations. To cry and complain about it is really unfair to these organizations. They, by design, cannot provide timely response to a tragedy. Organizations must have protocols and paperwork and checks and balances. They must have oversight and watchdogs to insure there is not theft of resources or abuse (by those helping or those they are helping).

People that work in organizations cannot maintain the sense of urgency that a flood victim has about the situation. Government workers do this day in and day out. It is their job. They see these catastrophes over and over, played out in hurricanes and fires and tornadoes. Many become desensitized to the suffering, struggle and frustration of the typical victim. For them, it legitimately so, is routine. How could it not be?

As this was playing out, there was an incredible, important reality. In Texas, mold does not wait! As FEMA and insurance companies were getting their organizations in place and deployed, mold was growing. As homeowners were calling the FEMA hotline and waiting on hold for HOURS, mold was growing. As insurance companies were figuring out how many adjusters they needed to move to the area, and how long they would need to be here, mold was growing! Homes had to be demoed ASAP!

Demoing is not a simple or easy process. The last thing we wanted to do was create worse damage or see someone who was helping get hurt. Demoing requires a team leader who knows what they are doing. Someone who can keep people from making mistakes, like cutting out sheetrock with a battery powered saw as they cut through all the electrical wiring in the wall! Demoing involves taking everything in the house that is growing mold to the curb. Electrical wiring doesn't grow mold, it can stay!

The vast majority of the 14,000 homes that were flooded in the greater Katy area lost everything that was on the first floor of their home. It sat in water for a few days in the Texas heat and was growing mold. And once mold is growing, it is nearly impossible to get rid of or destroy! The only thing to do is get rid of whatever is the mold carrier. Once furniture is out of the house, the walls, and everything inside them that mold could grow in (insulation, etc.) has to be removed up to four feet (if the water was over three feet then the walls are removed to the ceiling). All the flooring has to be taken out. Hardwood floors and even tile that has had water on it for that long is almost always growing mold underneath the beautiful tiles or hardwoods.

Doors, tile around fireplaces, and kitchen cabinets all had to be removed. Demoing is a job for a crew of about 15-20 and usually takes at least a day to do; a long day of backbreaking work. I love how Chip on Fixer Upper makes it look fun . . . . but its hard work (#DEMODAY)!

Churches all across the city were also making decisions about how they would respond. Most churches were taking seriously their responsibility to care for their church members. This, in itself, was an amazing thing. But, what about our neighbors who didn't attend a church? Who would help them?

Jerry, Glenn, and I met to talk through where we were and what we would do going forward. At this point, our rescue operation was completed. We were done running boats and getting people out of flood waters. In fact, that was pretty much a completed operation everywhere.

We were still hosting a "store" for those impacted. We were a major information hub (FEMA was using our facility for individual meetings and community wide meetings). We had a huge base of registered volunteers. We had teams out demoing houses over the weekend and today, people in our church helping their friends and neighbors. We had a significant number of flooded church members.

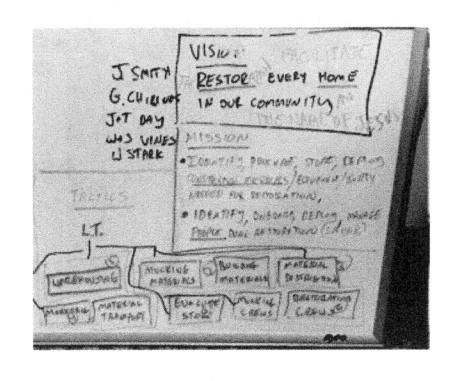

Over the last couple of days, in the midst of everything else we were doing on a whiteboard in my office, our team had identified a simple vision and several mission critical issues for the restoration phase of our response. The first step in that restoration phase was clearly this urgent need for the homes to be demoed and remediated for mold.

We had a simple working vision: "facilitating the restoration of every home in our community in the name of Jesus." We knew we needed to identify, procure, store, and deploy construction materials, equipment, and supplies needed for restoration. We would also need to identify, onboard, deploy, and manage people doing demo and restoration. We identified several mission critical items, such as warehousing, demoing/mucking materials, building materials, material distribution, marketing, material transportation, a store, administrative help, accounting, demoing crews, and restoration crews.

Jerry encouraged us to press on! At this point, we were building the train tracks as the train was barreling along.

Throughout the day, our team was coordinating demoing of homes and working on other mission critical items. Glenn and I headed to Kingsland Baptist Church to see what they were doing and learn from them.

Kingsland is another awesome church in Katy that Jerry has networked with for the last several years. They were working hard on Harvey efforts and had partnered with the Texas Baptist Men, the relief arm of Baptists in Texas. The Texas Baptist Men had helped with hurricane recovery in Texas and beyond for years. Men and women from all over Texas, many of them retired, give their time and energy to go and provide relief to devastated areas. It was truly an amazing sight to see what they had organized!

In one part of the parking lot, they were distributing boxes to anyone who drove up. This was a huge need as flood victims were getting into their homes and working through all their belongings on the first floor. They needed boxes for family heirlooms and memories that they wanted to try and salvage. They needed boxes and boxes for all the items they were going to throw to the curb.

In another part of the parking lot, they had cooking stations and trailers set up preparing meals for the Red Cross. Everyday, they cooked 10,000 meals that the Red Cross distributed across Houston, 5,000 lunches and 5,000 dinners. This was a huge undertaking and was running like an amazing, well-oiled machine.

In portable buildings, they had set up a command center for demoing homes ("mucking out" was a term they used that was new to me). There were various people developing maps and a database to track the status of the homes they were working with. They had a system for entering a new home needing help and tracking that help throughout the process of being demoed. At this point, they had completed seven homes in the area, but they were just ramping up.

The Baptist Men had team leaders who could go in and work with unskilled crews of volunteers demoing homes. These guys could also train other Team Leaders over time, especially if that person had somewhat of a construction background or was a "handy man" type.

Once a home is demoed, it must dry out sufficiently before the restoration process can continue. That usually involves industrial fans, cranking down the A/C as the electricity gets back on, and using a moisture meter to check the moisture levels in various spots. This can be a few days to a several week process, depending on how long the home stood in water or sat without being demoed.

The Texas Baptist Men also had teams that would go in after the home dried out, spray the home with mold remediation spray, and provide a certificate of that work. This certificate was critical, especially if the homeowner at some point down the road wanted to sell the home. In Texas, you don't want to buy a house that might have mold! This service was a huge blessing for many homeowners as companies charge hundreds of dollars to perform this simple task.

Our visit to Kingsland was very encouraging, The Texas Baptist Men and Kingsland were doing amazing things! After leaving, Glenn and I had conversations about how we should proceed. Should we just fold in and work with them? Should we run our own system and partner with them in various areas? There was never a question that we were going to do SOMETHING, it was a question of, "what will we do and how will we do it so that it is most effective?"

In the end, after talking with our team, we felt there was definitely a need for us to develop our own organization for many reasons. We had a highly motivated leadership team and a strong base of volunteers. We had contacts with a lot of churches who might not work with the Texas Baptist Men at that level. We had a significant number of our own members who needed help and deep contacts in the neighborhoods right around the church who were significantly impacted.

One thing we began to recognize was that if we were going to see the restoration of all the homes in greater Katy, we would have to have a system for finding out what homes were actually impacted. At this point, we were getting this info through word of mouth: directly from someone walking into the church or a friend of a friend who knew we were helping people and knew someone who was impacted. This was similar to the way we found out about people needing rescue.

We were fairly certain that, as the recovery progressed, the government would be contacted by everyone who was directly impacted. We also knew that the likelihood of the government sharing that list with a church was nil to none. If we were truly going to see our community completely restored, we would have to have a master list of people who were in need.

We talked with the team that had been working on forms through the rescue phase. John, our Worship Pastor, and Evan, one of our Tech Gurus, had put together some wonderful tools during that time. We asked what it would take to develop a self propagating form online that would merge into a database program that would electronically fill with information on those impacted. They said, "piece of cake," and began working on it. By the end of the day, we had an online form that an impacted neighbor could fill out with basic information, information that would flow directly into a database.

As we identified people who were impacted, we also wanted to give focused attention towards having a loving, hands on, "we are invested with you," "we are gonna treat you like an Auntie or Grandma who was impacted" relationship with them. We wanted to be incredibly customer focused, insuring that we were the HEART of Christ, as we grew a structure that was being the HANDS and FEET of Christ! "Over the top" customer service can only happen with intentionality and planning. Exceptional customer service requires a system that functions more like an organism than an organization. It is virtually impossible for a highly developed organization to compete with "grass roots" when it comes to service and care. Despite best intentions, everything about a highly evolved organization fights against human touch and emotion. We did not want to build a highly structured organization that fought against customer service.

To accomplish the "heart" component, we established what we eventually called "Care Coordinators." These were individuals who were the liaison between the organization we would develop and our hurting neighbors. Care Coordinators had the hard job of caring for the individual while pushing the helping structures we would develop to be responsive, timely, and caring. Rather than simply having people "get on a list," we wanted them to work with a real person who was committed to walking them through the entire process, from start to finish.

These Care Coordinators would need to be people of high emotional intelligence and empathy. They would be walking with someone through the devastation of throwing out grandma's piano or dragging to the curb the rocking chair they had nursed their children in. Care Coordinators would have to be able to push leaders of our various systems, to insure that we were delivering what we promised in a timely manner. We knew we were programming for conflict between the Care Coordinators and those actually doing the demoing and "hands on" stuff. We preferred this type of inter-organizational conflict to impacted neighbors NOT getting timely information or help. We wanted to be a warm, relational organism to our impacted neighbors, not a cold, impersonal institution.

Eventually, we had a list of 25 Care Coordinators. We asked each of them to take on five flood victims whom they would walk with through the restoration (similar to a Case Manager in Social Work). We felt that it would be difficult for someone to be a volunteer and provide care for more than that. We had our Care Coordinators contact neighbors on our list, to begin that hand holding process.

We also had an inkling that three or four weeks down the road volunteer motivation would diminish. This is understandable. In a life or death crisis, people are going to be urgently engaged in helping a friend who is worried for their safety as water is rising around them. At this point in our Harvey experience, we did not have this life or death urgency. Oh, it was very bleak and dire for those impacted, but it wasn't as if they faced imminent danger. We knew that it would feel even less and less dire for those of us not directly impacted in the weeks to come.

Couple this with everyone getting back to the grind of life and you can see how it ultimately became a struggle to provide help during this restoration stage. Over time, people who had been helping were experiencing "giving fatigue" and that was coupled with the pressures of their own life. After a rough several days, many who were helping just needed to disengage from the crisis.

We did have an amazing cadre of dedicated individuals who served over and over as the weeks went by. We also had incredible groups of people who came in from out of town. But, looking back, I wish we had leveraged the extensive volunteer list we had and foreseen the needs two, three, four weeks down the road. We really needed this base of volunteers four weeks into Harvey, when we were still finding neighbors with demo needs, but struggling to find the volunteers to go in and help.

We had another piece of awesome news as the day ended. Through a Facebook contact we connected with Cane Island Storage just north of Katy High School. They wanted to donate 3,000 square feet of mostly covered warehouse space. It was primarily designed for campers and RV's and we felt we could definitely adapt it to our use. John had worked the phones over the weekend and SunState Rental donated the use of a forklift and pallet jacks. We were on our way to warehousing resources as they came into the community!

While we had been planning for our future response, the team at the church was brilliantly executing caring for our community. FEMA was meeting at the church with individuals. Impacted neighbors were still being fed, supplied, and informed.

Throughout the day, Glenn and David had been coordinating teams out evaluating and demoing houses. We also had teams working in the homes of church members to demo them as well.

At various times throughout the day, Jayson, David and I worked with Glenn on our "Vision, Mission, Values and Strategy" elements. We hoped that other churches would partner with us and knew that would require clarity.

As we developed vision, mission, strategy, and values we worked hard to make sure that our vision was realistic and God sized. We did not want to fall into the trap that so many fall into about vision. The dangerous trap that vision is just some dream or BHAG (thanks, Jim Collins for your "Big Hairy Audacious Goal" acronym). For those with this limited view of vision, vision is just something you dream up because you will be "all good" if you get to within 20% or 30% of accomplishing the vision. We knew that our vision could not be some sort of motivational tool or catchy slogan.

We knew this because, in the end, vision, even a great vision, doesn't DO anything! It can't do anything. What gets things done are people with passion and the necessary resources! And when people, passion, and resources get coupled with a great vision and strategy, THAT can move mountains!

By themselves, vision statements and strategies do nothing. They are just words. But, coupled with motivated and empowered people AND a compelling need and story, an awesome vision and strategy can do great things!

To get to a true vision statement, there must be an honest assessment of current realities and current resources. Along with this, there must be a clear idea of where you want to be in five years. With these, you can come up with a statement of where you hope to end up. A vision statement is a clear, memorizable statement of the reason you live . . . your passion . . . . your drive for the next five years! That vision should flow out of your values and should, with a laser like focus, inform your structures and strategies.

As the day wound down, we updated people via social media regarding new needs we had identified based on our change in focus. We were shifting from primarily providing rescue and emergency care to assisting with demoing and clean up. We were taking the first step towards our restoration vision!

At around 8:30 PM, I got to practice my Care Coordinator skills as I talked on the phone with the husband I talked with in the copy room on Sunday, the one I had promised that we were committed to walking with them throughout their Harvey experience. I was able to share the info I learned from our visit to Kingsland about mold and the process they were facing. I prayed with him and, over the next couple of days, walked with their family as their house got demoed.

Leadership Lesson #27 - Leaders figure out how to stay connected directly in customer service. They know that the skills necessary for providing excellent customer service erode over time if they are not practiced. Good Leaders are committed to retaining them!

TUESDAY

September 5 - Organization or Organism?

Early Tuesday morning, we went public with our vision and strategy for the restoration phase. Our goal was to let those in our community know where we were headed. We also hoped other churches would partner with us in accomplishing this vision. We felt that, given what our church and community

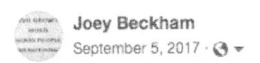

Joey Beckham
September 5, 2017

The Fellowship in Katy is looking for churches to partner with to do this. Let's dream big and do it together!

Vision - Through the power of Jesus facilitate the restoration of every home in the greater Katy area.

Mission:
1. Identify, procure, store, and deploy construction materials, equipment, and supplies needed for restoration.
2. Identify, onboard, deploy, and manage people doing restoration.
3. Do this all with a grassroots neighbor oriented structure that is HIGH touch for our neighbors who have been impacted (A Touch Point Person will take their hand and walk them all the way through the process).

Mission Critical Teams (need a high capacity point person for each):
1. Mucking crews and Restoration crews
2. Mucking materials and Restoration materials
3. IT, Admin, Marketing, etc.
4. Evacuee Store or a system for evacuees to access resources
5. Warehousing, material transport, material distribution
6. Centralized database that can be populated organically that will identify each Neighbor impacted and track our delivery of services through restoration.

Key values:
1. We want to keep the personal touch. As agencies take over they become less neighborly and personal. We want to keep at the forefront the reality that these are our neighbors throughout the process. Our NEIGHBORS have been impacted mightily.
2. We don't care who gets the credit!
3. We want our community rebuilt even better than it was!
4. We want to be decentralized, not centralized. Sure we need structures and procedures but we want a flat organization that delivers.
5. If someone is doing it better FOR OUR COMMUNITY we will let them run with it. Before we let them run with it we will first verify that they are truly doing it better. We won't just take their word for it, we want to see that they are doing it!
6. We don't want to become a relief agency. We are a Church . . . who wants to provide relief for our members and our community. Jesus has got to be central.
7. Resources are flowing through our community like crazy. We want to capture the ones that will help with recovery and ask for the right things from folks who are out of town.
8. Do I believe that God is big enough to accomplish this vision?
9. We are committed to using the resources we receive with integrity. In many disasters the people impacted by the disaster don't really get much tangible benefit. Many resources are stolen and wasted. We won't let this happen because we belong to Jesus and we truly want to help our neighbors.

Please reach out to me if you want to join in this God sized vision!

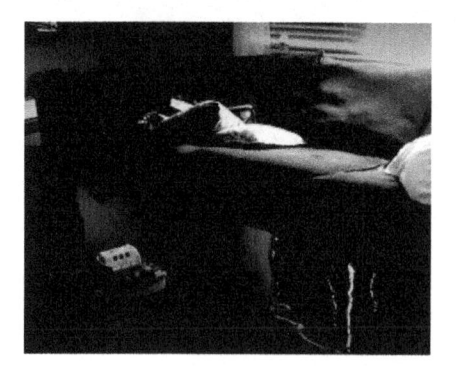

had done, this was not unrealistic or just a pipe dream.

Impacted neighbors were coming in looking for help with clean up and volunteers were coming in looking for places to help. We tried our best to identify Team Leaders who could facilitate evaluating homes and insuring that no damage was done as we were helping clean up.

The first step, though, for everyone impacted was taking detailed and extensive pictures of the damage. For FEMA and insurance documentation, before our flooded neighbors moved anything, they had to catalogue what was damaged.

Next was the difficult step of deciding what they were going to try to salvage and what they were going to put on the curb for trash. This was a heart breaking process for many of them. As best we could, we partnered at least one person from the church with the emotional capacity to go with them and walk with them through this difficult experience.

I distinctly remember one lady who came in looking for people to help her clean out her house. We had several folks from the community there to volunteer. I asked for volunteers who were willing to get dirty and maybe move some heavy stuff. A teenager and a couple of ladies raised their hands. I put them with the lady needing help. As we were standing in the foyer, one of our church Elders came walking in the door. He was retired from the school district and an amazing servant. I asked him what he was doing and he said he was there to volunteer. I said, "here is the team for you."

We prayed together before they went out. When we were done, one of the ladies looked up and said, "and down the road we can help this lady because her house was flooded as well." Imagine that, her home was flooded and here she was volunteering to help someone else clean out their house!

I also began working with my Principal, Dr. Rice, to determine my transition back to work. Teachers were due back on Wednesday and she very graciously gave me permissions to flex my school time over the next few days around all the work I was doing in the community.

She asked me to share what had been going on with the staff and pray for us. If you remember, McMeans is one of the locations where we had been assisting neighbors coming out of the flood waters. They had been dropping boats into the water in front of our parking lot! This would be our first time back in the building since all this began.

Dr. Rice also asked me to help coordinate a work day for our school to serve in the community. Our district again did the right thing, and asked all the staff to get in the community on Friday, helping our co-workers and students who were impacted by the flood.

At the church we put together a script for volunteer follow-up. Unfortunately, in all the work of the next few days, with school and clean up teams and the needs of flood victims, this element did not get implemented at the level we would have liked. We really dropped the ball by not leveraging the thousands of registered volunteers we had in our database!

> Thanks for calling people today. As we shift from our recovery to restoration stage, we need to call all our volunteers and touch base. Thousands of people signed up during the disaster and we want to thank them and let them know our needs going forward.
>
> Here is a general script for your conversation. If you get voicemail please leave this as a message.
>
> Hi! I'm _____ from The Fellowship. You signed up to volunteer during the rescue phase of our work. THANKS FOR HELPING! As we move to our recovery phase our vision is that through the power of Jesus we will facilitate the restoration of every home in the greater Katy area. This is a God size vision and we need everyone's help!
>
> I have a few questions for you:
>
> 1. Was your home impacted by the flood? **If yes:** how can we help you?? **If no:** thanks for pitching in to help our neighbors!
> 2. We would love for you to commit to help going forward. Here are places we have need:
>   1. Mud out (some call this "demo") homes - crews who will work with our Team Leaders. You will get in and do hard, tear out work (16 years or old).
>   2. Team Leaders for these crews.
>   3. People to help pack and move people out of their homes.
>   4. Transportation for people and supplies (adults only).
>   5. People to make food for National Guard still stationed here.
>   6. Host homes for people responding here from out of town.
>
> Where are three places you could help?
>
> **If they say, I am super busy or need to go back to work, say:** No problem, we are trying to gear this up for folks who have to get back to their life. We want people to be able to help as they can. Even if you could only work a 4 hour shift it could be a HUGE help!
>
> Thanks for serving our community! Working together we are going to get through this!!

Jayson, David, Glenn, and I continued to work on the vision and strategy. We also

---

Leadership Lesson #28 - Leaders honestly evaluate experiences, events, or interactions to learn from them. We all make mistakes, leaders learn from their mistakes.

began to reach out to contacts that might play a key role in the structure, and churches that might participate with us as well.

One concern we had as we began fleshing out the vision and strategy was insuring that we did not lose the fluidity and adaptability of an organism as we built an organization. Typically, things that become highly organized become less effective. In the church world, it is common knowledge that as a church grows, its percentage of baptism and growth year-over-year diminishes. And it diminishes significantly.

Organizations become bureaucratic and bureaucracies become more concerned about protecting the organization than fulfilling a compelling vision. Bureaucracies create silos where people can easily point the finger of blame at others in the bureaucracy for why they are not effective, which further diminishes the effectiveness of the organization. In fact, you often never truly know the effectiveness of an organization because each silo is allowed to define "success" as they see fit. Then, that silo exaggerates their own success and expend amazing amounts of energy defending themselves against other silos, rather than accomplishing much around the vision.

Organisms keep an intense focus on results and the bottom line. Organisms have the ability to reproduce. Bureaucracies tend to grow fatter and more bloated.

Our passion, as we built our Restoration Response, was that we help as many of our neighbors as possible by growing as an organized, life-giving organism and not becoming a cold, sterile, "blame shifting" bureaucratic organization.

Leadership Lesson #29 - Leaders give a lot of energy and effort towards keeping their organization flat. The further away one gets from the delivery point, the front lines, the less ability they have to make timely, effective customer oriented dec9 decisions.

Glenn Lerich
Tue 9/5/2017, 10:06 PM
Wayne ████████████████<███████████et>; Joey Beckham

Flag for follow up. Start by Wednesday, October 18, 2017. Due by Wednesday, October 18, 2017.

You forwarded this message on 9/6/2017 9:23 PM

My recommendations after recap from Doug ████ and Robert ██████ after Kelly home.

Home Owner Must Do's Prior to Team demo. Find a way to send to each family on our list.
1) take video- room by room, wall by wall, of damage.
2) take pictures of furniture damaged.
3) identify items to save vs trash so decisions don't have to be made on the fly
4) a full cell phone battery and space on their phone so more pictures and videos can be taken as walls are opened.
5) any items in lower cupboards and closets that's going to be saved needs to be moved higher or out, so you can assume everything below the water line is trash
6) identify a space away from a wall and make room in that space for saved items - garage, back patio, etc. items can be moved back inside once demo is done.
7) electricity and gas turned off
8) figure out if they want certain hardware saved - door handles, cabinet pulls, etc.

New criteria:
1) No team goes without pre-assessment.
2) No assessor or teams into areas with street flooding   3) Assessor needs to confirm owner has done all insurance filing before starting work.   4) If cabinets are assessed for removal houses need to be packed before a team goes.   5) 1st aide kit for every teams   5) Teams wear minimum of N99 Dust masks.
6) Begin developing 10 team Kit per our current list. Assume team will be 10 people.

WEDNESDAY

September 6 - Demo Is The First Step To Restoration

Katy ISD did amazing things for the community during Harvey—setting up shelters, opening their facilities to First Responders, juggling their own damaged facilities, teachers and administration out serving the community as we were "off" from school. Like the community response to Harvey, the response of the district was unprecedented!

But, like Sunday for churches, Mondays for teachers are always around the corner (except during the blessed summertime). Today, teachers were asked to report back to their schools to get ready for our second "first day of class" of the year, Monday, September 11. Harvey hit barely a week into school, so for everyone, coming back after Harvey was like starting fresh.

McMeans is a well-oiled machine and I work with an amazing team of administrators and teachers. As a staff of about 90, we serve around 1100 6-8th graders. Our school was just on the edge of the flood zone east of The Fellowship. In fact, its parking lot had been one of the main extraction points for the area a week ago. Boats to go into the flooded neighborhoods were being launched from the parking lot of McMeans!

Dr. Rice and I had worked out that I would float from church to school doing the best I could to continue my relief efforts through the church while getting ready for students on Monday.

We met together as a school staff and I shared for about 35 minutes what had been going on in our area and gave a mini-presentation on Harvey. Dr. Rice talked through logistics for the week and we began coordinating the district required "get out and help in Harvey" day on Friday.

As we began to organize our efforts for Friday, it became very evident that our amazing choir teacher, Steve Kalke, had been in the thick of Harvey response as well, especially when the clean up and demo of houses began.

The Mormon church has an amazing disaster response organization called Helping Hands. The last few days, as I had been out in neighborhoods helping organize clean up and demoing, I had seen teams of people in yellow shirts working together as well. It was so awesome to see them walk up to a house with a skilled Team Lead and a crew and offer to help any way they could. Steve had been working closely with them and their efforts.

Steve dove in with me on organizing how we would help our school community. We had a sign up sheet in the break room, one for "I Need Help" and another for "Here Is How I Will Help On Friday." While we did not have much information on impacted students, we did identify eight homes of our colleagues that needed help in one way or another.

Every available staff member volunteered to help on Friday. Some helped with administration at the school, some with food onsite, some with getting lunch kits put together for everyone going out. Many others signed up to go into homes and do whatever it took to help them take the next step towards recovery. For those impacted, at this point, it was one step at a time, one day at a time. As I tell my students at school when I assign a big project, "how do you eat an elephant?" "One bite at a time!"

As Steve and I began working on this, I got in my classroom and had a quick meeting with Lee Anne and Jon, my amazing teammates for 8th Grade US History. Jon had been one of the first guys to show up at Cinco Ranch High School when we were organizing as a shelter despite juggling his young family's needs during the disaster. Lee Ann, Jon, and I have worked together at McMeans for several years and truly love one another and love working together. They volunteered to carry the load on class prep so I could give time and energy to continued organization of efforts at the church and for our work day at McMeans.

At the church, we were phasing out our "store" and transitioning our focus to the Restoration Phase, and at this point specifically clean up and demoing. We continued matching volunteers with impacted neighbors who needed clean up.

Our church staff was working hard to identify competent volunteers who could take over the roles they had been filling so capably. Overall leadership of the response going forward was being transferred to Glenn.

Carly and John continued working on warehouse space. They finalized things with Cane Island Storage, who donated a huge amount of partially enclosed space and two enclosed units as well. It was amazing! SunState delivered the forklift and pallet jacks as promised. This was a giant step towards our vision of walking impacted neighbors through their entire Harvey experience: rescue, clean up, demoing, and rebuilding.

Today was also a bittersweet day as we said goodbye to the National Guard unit that had been housed at the church for the last several days. While we were glad that the rescue phase of things was over, we had bonded deeply with these awesome

First Responders. These Guardsmen (and women) had worked alongside us in our community as we struggled to rescue people and began the clean up process. They had helped us move stuff, been wet and cold with us, protected us, loved on people, and cared for us and our neighbors. We had shared many meals together. The National Guard had become an integral part of our Harvey Family. It was sad to see them go!

On their way out of town, we put them to work one last time. We were closing down our store at the church and they graciously helped transport a huge load of supplies to our new warehouse space. Once again, Carly and her Jeep came in handy as she led them in another one of the thousands of ways they helped our community.

Jayson, David, and I continued to work on the vision and strategy. We identified key processes and developed an organizational chart for this new phase. Jayson worked on getting everything together for a presentation with Jerry and Dave, our Church Administrator. The rescue phase had been a 100 yard dash, this would be a marathon!

People began to commit to key roles in our organizational structure going forward (at least the structure as it stood). Wayne, a former Sheriff and all around handy man was tapped to give leadership to our demo teams and team leads. Joel, a former Army Ranger and businessman, who himself had been impacted, committed to overseeing our warehouse. Carly, who was working on her Master's in Social Work, took leadership over our Care Coordinators. Diane, who was coming back home from out of town and had helped start a relief organization in Katy several years earlier (Compassion Katy), volunteered to help us liaison with other churches for this Restoration phase of the process. Jennifer, a wonderful church member with amazing capacity, took on the huge job of coordinating our out of town volunteers. Gabriel, an amazing church member and young businessman from Brazil, who had some free time for a couple of months, was willing to step into my support role over time as I transitioned back to teaching and my part-time responsibilities as Groups Pastor at the church.

We took over the Community Room in the main building as our Command Center for the demo stage. Wayne and his Assistant, Garry, began organizing food and tools for teams that were heading out to work in homes. Eventually, half the room was filled with the necessary items to get the initial clean up completed. More sophisticated tools, like power tools and floor strippers, would come later. Right now teams needed brooms, shovels, trash bags and a lot of muscle to move furniture and soaked memories from the first floors of homes.

On the way home that night, I called an impacted neighbor who had filled out one of our forms. Audrey shared her story of working to recover. She also mentioned, with love and grace, that someone at the church had told her that someone would be by today to check their home and no one showed up. We had broken Leadership Lesson #22 . . . . we had over-promised and under-delivered!

At our church, we have a life-changing discipleship program called Faithwalking, it trains us in owning our mistakes and "cleaning up" our emotional messes. Dropping the ball with Audrey was a place where I really had to put my Faithwalking skills to practice! I apologized profusely and made a personal commitment to walk with her, as her Care Coordinator, to help her navigate our newly developing organization. We discussed getting a team to her home to help with the clean up and demo of the house and I prayed with her as we hung up. This experience reinforced our commitment to have Care Coordinators who served as a buffer between impacted neighbors and our demo teams.

We quickly began coordinating out of town teams into the area. We had several from North Texas. One that I built an ongoing relationship with was our Community Beer Team from Dallas. I don't even know how she got my contact info, but I got an email from Andi out of the blue. This awesome company worked with us, bringing crew after crew to serve our community, until the day we stopped demoing houses.

Ready to serve

Andi Carr <andi@communitybeer.com>
Wed 9/6/2017 3:38 PM
Joey Beckham

You replied on 9/6/2017 9:35 PM

Hi Joey,

My name is Andi, and I live in Dallas now, but I grew up in the Houston area. My husband and I and a few others are coming to your area to help with the recovery efforts this weekend. Would you possibly have some work for us?

Please let me know.

Thank you,

Andi Carr

Community Beer Company
1530 Inspiration Drive, Ste 200
Dallas, Texas 75207

Beer For the Greater Good

Leadership Lesson #30 - Leaders treat everyone with respect. They know that every person they encounter and every conversation they have has the potential to be a life changing benefit for them. They may be entertaining angels, unaware!

THURSDAY

September 7 - Systems and Structures

Demoing usually began around 7:30 AM and crews were working until late at night. I began the day coordinating various demo jobs while juggling getting ready for school and a very important meeting with Jerry and the team to discuss how we were progressing and where we were headed.

Earlier in the week, I randomly met Gary who had a background in construction and dove in wherever he could. It was awesome to connect people in need with folks who assisted them in amazing ways. By the end of the day, Gary had helped two of our neighbors take significant strides in demoing their homes and I had him lined up to help Audrey the next morning.

The way people sacrificed was truly incredible. I had an unexpected need for a pickup truck. One of the guys who showed up to help demo, whom I didn't even really know, lent me his truck for most of the day and rode with someone else to the home they were working in! The hearts of people to help was inspiring!

On Wednesday night, Jayson, David, and I finalized a presentation for Jerry. We wanted to apprise him of what was going on and give clarity to how we felt we should move forward. Dave, our Church Administrator, would be there as well. Dave was getting up to speed at this point after being out of town during the rescue phase. He would be helping with the financial side of things for our Harvey Response going forward.

We made significant strides towards a workable vision and structure for what we were calling Restore Katy. Ultimately, we wanted to partner with our neighbors in getting their houses rebuilt. A key word in this is "partner." We wanted to help our impacted neighbors help themselves. Often, as I talked about demoing their home, I would encourage them to get their friends and family members there to help, to gather a helping team as we were gathering a team to help them. We knew that assisting our neighbors would take a variety of forms depending on their circumstance (information, money, construction crews, a place to stay, ???).

We also wanted to partner with other churches in this endeavor. We were already working closely with several churches and felt that what we were doing was scaleable to many churches working together to get the job done.

People in the community were in various stages of recovery and had varied mitigating circumstances. About 15% had flood insurance which was a significant help. FEMA was going to come in and give some help to the 85% of people who did not have flood insurance. For some, the help from FEMA would be significant. I know of one family in Bear Creek whose home was completely underwater after they escaped. The entire home! FEMA gave them $250,000 for the total loss of their home and they made money when they sold the lot.

For the vast majority, though, the help from FEMA was not enough, by a large amount. Others in our community had planned well and had the financial resources to do a lot of the restoration themselves. Sadly, there were others who had no help at all. As I write this in July 2018, of the approximately 14,000 homes that were flooded in the greater Katy area (six zip codes), there are about 2,000 homes that have done very little in the rebuild process.

As we thought through what we wanted to accomplish, we believed that, with God's help, we could create a system that would insure that all impacted homes in our area got rebuilt one way or another (volunteers and donations, FEMA, flood insurance, homeowners resources). This was obviously a God sized vision! It would require a lot of sacrificial work and a lot of cooperation on the part of churches. It would also likely be a year or more to see it to completion.

We knew that one key pinch point for this vision was actually knowing who needed help. We believed that, down the road, the government would have some type of database that would have this information, but there were a couple of problems.

One problem was that the information, if it came to us from the government, would likely be AFTER the need. People were in significant need right now! We also knew that if we depended on the government for this information, in the end, it was highly unlikely that they would even give us the information! Due to privacy laws and the way the government handles information dissemination on a "need-to-know" basis, it was very unlikely that a bunch of churches would ever get this information from them.

We felt we had a good solution around these problems. Earlier in the process, we had adapted forms from the Texas Baptist Men and impacted neighbors physically filled these out as they came into the church or we filled

Leadership Lesson #31 - Leaders identify the pinch points of the organization, the key issues that keep them from taking significant strides, and attack them with a vengeance!

the form out when they called in on the phone. John, our Worship Pastor, and Evan, our Tech Guru had developed a simple online fillable form that would feed information into a master database. An impacted neighbor now could use this online form to give us basic information on who they were and what they needed. Using social media we felt that this web based form would be a way to get contact info on everyone in the greater Katy area who had been impacted and had a need.

Our vision was also that one way we would partner with other churches in the restoration phase would be by giving limited access to this database to a key person in that church. As impacted neighbors filled out the form online, the information would go into the master database. The information could be viewed by individuals at the partnering churches. A church could then adopt an impacted neighbor in their immediate area (or specific neighbors the church wanted to help). That church would then take responsibility for that family throughout the rebuild process (or as far as they could take them).

Demoing flooded houses over the last few days had given insight into the process and what we would be doing for the next several weeks. Demoing a home involved the following steps:

- Get safe
- Contact insurance and FEMA right away
- Take pictures and video of everything impacted
- Determine what must be removed from the house and get it out
- Keep taking pictures and video
- As soon as possible crank the A/C down as low as feasible and get fans circulating the air to start drying out the house.
- Remove sheetrock, baseboard, and anything else in the walls (not pipes or electric). It should be removed at four feet if the interior wall is dry above that level. It should be removed to the ceiling if it is wet above four feet (sheetrock is most easily installed at four feet and eight feet lengths). Sometimes, if it is only a few inches of water, the walls can be removed lower than four feet.
- Usually, any cabinets that sat in water must be removed. The wall behind the cabinet will grow mold. You can try to save counter tops when they come off, but it is hard to do. Sinks can be left in.
- Most flooring has to come out. Tile and hardwood floors were big question marks for homeowners early in the demo process because they are

expensive. In the significant percentage of instances, they had to come out of the house eventually.

- Wash all the exposed studs and the floors with a pressure washer.
- Let the house dry out. This usually involved industrial fans throughout the house and A/C very low. Use moisture meters to insure levels throughout the house are below the acceptable levels. Moisture measurements must be taken in various locations.
- Spray all exposed studs in the house with a mold remediation formula. This was an awesome service that the Texas Baptist Men provided free of charge while "for profit" companies were doing it for $700-900.
- Begin the rebuilding process AFTER insurance and/or FEMA approval.

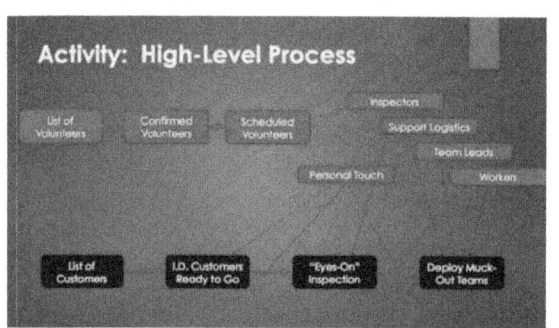

At the meeting with Pastor Jerry and Dave, Jayson shared the vision and the presentation we had worked on with clarity and simplicity. We were ultimately creating an organization that would manage volunteers serving impacted neighbors (our customers). At this point, we were focused mainly on the demo (or muck out) phase because we knew that every impacted neighbor would have to go through this process prior to beginning reconstruction. The Demo Phase takes 5-7 weeks (or more) to get through.

We had already begun building an amazing organization around this vision, with high capacity people in various roles. Today, we added Dave into the Finance role and another key person, Dexter, to our warehouse operations.

Jerry and Dave had some great questions and input. One key concern was that we make sure we clearly identify critical needs and get our volunteers working directly on those needs. We wanted to get as much laser focus on the critical item we were delivering for the next several weeks, demoing houses. When the words **"Time on Tools"** came up, all the business guys in the meeting sat straight up with a slight grin on their faces.

Essentially, we wanted to insure that as much **TIME** as possible was focused with hands on **TOOLS** that were delivering the most important work, **DEMOING**! We knew that this weekend would be very informative as we had a large base of volunteers coming in to help demo houses.

While we were meeting, Carly finalized a script for our Care Coordinators to use as they made their initial contact. A key part of our vision was maintaining a caring, loving heart as our demoing organization grew. These amazing people took on the incredibly difficult job of walking alongside people in the midst of their pain. It was very easy for those of us in the fast paced environment of clean up to lose sight of the human being we were helping. Our Care Coordinators made sure our impacted neighbors felt the love of Christ in this difficult process. They were there to insure that our

Initial Contact Script

Hi this is _____ from The Fellowship. You filled out a Southern Baptist Disaster Relief form on _____ and I'm following up. Has any other organization committed to Mud Out your home?

If YES – Who? _____ Can I pray for you?
If NO – Does your home currently have water in it?
If YES – as soon the water is out of your home, call me back to schedule an assessment.
    If NO – Can we drive to your house without hitting water?
        If YES – Can we schedule an assessment?
        If NO – Call me back to schedule an assessment.
Can I pray for YOU?

Care Coordinator - FAQs

INSURANCE
If they have insurance, provide them with our contact to help them get the ball rolling
    -Brian Holt ███████
    -We will not be helping those who are covered with flood insurance.
If they **DO NOT** have insurance, inquire about FEMA

FEMA (FEDERAL EMERGENCY MANAGEMENT AGENCY)
If someone does not have insurance they should talk to FEMA.
If they have not applied with FEMA, they need to do so ASAP. Link below:
https://www.fema.gov/apply-assistance

DEMO PROCESS
Once they have applied with FEMA and before we will send a crew out to help, they need to make sure **ALL** of the following items have been taken care of:
- Take video, room by rom, wall by wall, of the damage
- Take pictures of furniture damaged
- Identify items to save vs trash so decisions don't have to be made on the spot
- A full cell phone battery and space on their phone so more pictures and videos can be taken as walls are opened
- Any items in lower cupboards and closets that are going to be saved need to be moved higher or out, so you can assume everything below the water line is trash
- Identify a space away from a wall and make room in that space for saved items - garage, back patio, etc. Items can be moved back inside once demo is completed
- Electricity and gas turned off
- Decide if certain hardware should be saved - door handles, cabinet pulls, etc.

impacted neighbors did not get "lost" as our reconstruction organization developed.

Things at the school were coming together for our work in the community on Friday. Steve had outlined an awesome plan of action that took into consideration the fluid nature of demoing and clean up. Even now, almost two weeks after the flooding, it was vital to keep an attitude of flexibility because things could change by the moment! Others at McMeans were busy procuring tools, arranging transportation, organizing lunches, and doing prep work at the flooded homes.

Jon and Lee Anne had things ready for the following week in class. Monday would be an interesting day, given that it was 9/11 and, much like 9/11, we had experienced a major disaster in our area.

Back at the church, later that evening, I met with Gabriel. He was from Brazil and in a job transition, and he had a couple of months to donate to our efforts. My hope was that he would step into my role as I ultimately transitioned back into teaching US History and being the Groups Pastor at The Fellowship.

Carly Kirk
September 7, 2017

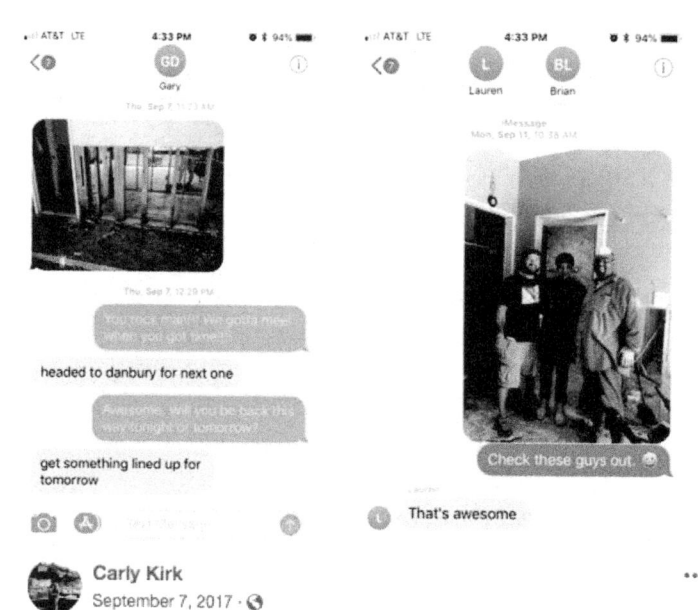

"Through waters uncharted my soul will embark// I'll follow Your voice straight into the dark// And if from the course You intend I depart// Speak to the sails of my wandering heart."

For the past month, Hillsong's 'Captain' has been my go to quiet time song. The last 10 days these words have resonated in my heart in a new, real, and deep way. I have been reminded of the role of our Captain. Our God is powerful and mighty, and He is love and hope. He has been present in the rescue and relief, and He will be present as we move towards recovery and restoration.

Leadership Lesson #32 - Leaders make sure they are keeping the main thing . . . . THE . . . . main thing!

FRIDAY - SATURDAY

September 8 and September 9 - Demoing, Demoing, Demoing

Friday was one of the proudest memories I have as a Katy ISD teacher. The staff of McMeans showed up at 7:00 AM ready to get to work! Steve provided maps to the location for their initial demo assignment for each team. He also had a secondary place to help if they got finished at their initial home. We got out the door and the teams began cleaning and demoing. Steve and I floated between the various locations making sure everyone had what they needed.

At the same time the McMeans staff was out, I was coordinating with other demo teams from The Fellowship who were in the area working on homes. Wayne and others at the church were busy identifying homes that were ready for teams and mobilizing teams out to those homes as team leads and volunteers showed up.

Over the last few days we had learned to ask the owner to take the initial step of consolidating everything they planned on keeping into one location before our demo crew showed up. This allowed us to focus the precious time of our volunteers on the hard work of moving trashed items to the curb and demoing.

For many impacted neighbors, identifying what they would keep and what they would trash was a much more time consuming process than they expected. Many items they picked up represented some cherished memory. They found themselves with the difficult task of weighing the value of the memory in the item they held against the cost and time to try to recover the item.

One unanticipated problem from the flood were the hundreds and hundreds of cars that were in mint condition, but absolutely unusable. Many people who had gotten out ahead of the flooding left at least one of their cars in the safety of their garage, never thinking that they would be flooded. Those who had gotten out on boats after the water rose, often had multiple cars in the garage or driveway that were now a total loss!

Already, insurance agencies were

83

sending tow trucks into the neighborhoods to pick up cars. Where the cars went when they left the neighborhood, no one knew. Often, the tow truck drivers had to push the car out of the garage or driveway and onto the street before he could tow it. On Friday, their presence, as well as the presence of homeowners and volunteers, made traffic pretty bad, even by Houston standards.

I cannot imagine what it was like, emotionally, to go back into these neighborhoods and homes for those who had flooded. The neighborhoods looked like scenes from a war zone. Houses in utter disarray. Piles and piles of furniture, clothes, and household items on the lawn in front of almost every yard. 10 feet high worth of stuff that covered the front yard to the curb!

I was having significant emotions stirring up as I drove around areas where just a few short days ago I had been riding in a boat looking for people to rescue. I took a picture at an intersection that had been under water by five feet or more where I had been riding in a boat a few days prior.

Canyon Gate is a community of over 700 homes that we did a lot of work in. This community was a mere three miles from The Fellowship and all but a handful of the homes flooded. I checked in on Audrey, where Gary was doing some preliminary work along with others. Her neighbor, Connie, attended our church and Audrey had visited the church with Connie a few times. Audrey was the gracious woman we had "over promised" and "under delivered" to. Mike was a neighbor of Audrey's, a few doors down. He had flooded, had already demoed his home himself, and was helping as many of his neighbors as he could. He had a construction background and did a great job organizing his neighbors to help one another.

John and Amy lived around the corner. They were the couple staying with Jayson throughout all this. They had another good friend named Duke who came into town from Las Vegas periodically to help them through the demo and reconstruction process. Duke eventually organized two friends who each donated an 18 wheel trailer load of sheetrock!

While we were demoing homes for the school and the church, I checked in with other homes in the area to see how they were doing. Many people were just now getting into their home and assessing the damage and what to do. Most had friends and family helping in the clean up process. Some had other volunteer crews like ours helping them significantly.

Home after home after home, every home on the street, was flooded. It was the rare exception to come across a home that was not a beehive of activity. Friends and family who were not impacted were doing whatever they could to help. Every street had teams of volunteers, from the Texas Baptist to the Mormon Helping Hands, walking around diving in and helping. Many of these teams had skilled demo Team Leaders who organized crews working in one home as they floated to other homes to assess the need.

Construction companies from various cities and states were also driving around looking for places to help, or maybe people to scam, we weren't quite sure. Going forward, one of the most difficult parts of recovery was finding reputable, honest construction companies to work with.

Those who had money, hired remediation companies who were working hard to get homes protected from the moisture and the

Leadership Lesson #33 - Leaders are able to find that delicate balance: they get out of their "Ivory Towers" and down in the trenches WITHOUT getting dragged into "The Weeds" and the minutia of day to day operations. They are both in AND above the battle!

mold. Amazingly, there were still homes that had not even opened their front door: people on vacation when the hurricane hit, renters who abandoned the home, even some who had left the country for the summer and weren't expected back for several weeks. Whatever the reason, these homes had been sitting unopened for over a week after the waters receded!

Clearly, our work was urgent. We anticipated there would be 7-8 weeks of active demoing. Homes that did nothing until that time would likely have mold in every nook and crevice. There would be no way to salvage anything in the home. Even the integrity of the structure would be in question!

By the end of the day, our McMeans crews had cleaned out the first floor of seven homes and had begun demoing several of them. We celebrated what we had done back at the school at the end of the day. Most of us headed home to a hot shower. Our flooded colleagues headed back to work some more on their homes.

Our teams at The Fellowship continued working until dark and then we planned for Saturday. We anticipated having four crews of 15 or so out in neighborhoods responding to needs. Others from the church would be out in the homes of friends and family members helping. Many church members would be in their OWN flooded homes working furiously.

Our plan on Saturday was for Aaron, Jennifer, and I to be in the neighborhood as feet on the ground organizing the work. Wayne, Carly, and others would be at the church, coordinating logistics and addresses for the teams. We had many homes close to each other and knew we could quickly get from one house to the next. A team of 10-15 hardworking volunteers can accomplish a lot towards demoing a home in four or five hours.

Saturday was a much more hectic day in the neighborhoods. The traffic was horrific with homeowners, volunteers, sightseers, tow truck drivers, remediation crews, and security personnel clogging the streets. John and I went to the Canyon Gate area to coordinate our work there. Aaron, another Pastor at The Fellowship and Jennifer, our out-of-town volunteer coordinator, were also helping manage crews in the community.

As we drove down Mason Road, we realized there was a line of traffic 1/2 mile long to get into the neighborhood. We parked in the neighborhood across the street and walked into Canyon Gate. I had a gracious, but pointed conversation with the security guard at the gate. I encouraged him to get the President of the Homeowners Association on the phone and let them know the chaos they were causing for people trying to come into the neighborhood to attend to the catastrophe. By requiring people to stop at the one lane entrance and give their ID and the address they were going to, they were making it impossible to help! Thankfully, later that day they were simply glancing at license plates and jotting them down quickly as people drove into the neighborhood.

Throughout the day, John and I walked from one end of the subdivision to the other multiple times. We probably logged eight miles of walking that day. Those who drove found it much more frustrating having to navigate around the maze of cars, tow trucks, and people in the community. One person told me it took them 30 minutes to drive from the home where they were helping to the front of the neighborhood!

The visuals were astounding. High water marks on the sides of homes at three or four feet. Brick walls that divided the homes from the main street laying in piles of rubble. Pools of water still in low spots in the road. Soggy yards that smelled like rotting vegetation. Mountains of trash in front of every house. The roads covered with two or three inches of dried mud. Cars and trucks everywhere, with most streets down to one lane. Tow trucks dragging cars out of the neighborhood. Every home with 10-15 masked people working furiously!

John and I stayed in close contact with the various teams in the neighborhood, as well as Glenn and Carly back at The Fellowship. As we walked around, we were able to give a personal contact to many on our list in the community and others that we met. Our crews did amazing things that day. Moving furniture, helping push cars out of garages that were flooded, tearing out sheetrock, bringing a smile to someone's overwhelmed face as the crew got a weeks worth of work done in four or five hours, giving hope to someone who didn't know how they would do it!

As we were floating around, I couldn't pass up taking this picture from the wall of John and Amy's home. They were a little further along than many in their neighborhood, already working on the demo process. On one of their walls, with four feet of the sheetrock torn out, was written, "Trust in the LORD with all your heart" in beautiful calligraphy. That saying had been written when they built their house, and had been hidden behind a picture hung on the wall. What an awesome reminder that, no matter our circumstances, the LORD is present with us!

By the end of the day on Saturday, we had moved the first floor furniture out of three homes and demoed six other homes.

We ended the day lining up locations for the teams to work on Sunday. As a leadership team at the church, we knew that we couldn't NOT respond on Sunday, despite our strong conviction that Sabbath rest is important. At this point, our neighbor's ox was in the proverbial ditch and we had to help!

Jayson and I put the final touches on a more polished vision and strategy for Restore Katy. Jerry and I had a meeting scheduled on Sunday to discuss how things could look going forward.

SUNDAY - SATURDAY
September 10 through September 16 - Back To Normal?

Today marked the two week anniversary of our Harvey experience. For most of the people in our community, this had been one of the most trying two weeks in their life! Sunday morning, Jerry shared a very encouraging, transparent message of where many of us were. Tired, but not out. Emotionally on edge, but learning to lean on God. Knowing that things would not be the same for a long while, if ever, and wondering what the new normal was going to look like.

After services, John and I again spent the day in the neighborhoods coordinating our efforts. Things were much less hectic today. Our two out of town teams, Community Beer and another church group from Decatur, Texas, worked as long as they could before heading home. We had various teams out helping from the church as well.

I also felt the need to get with Jerry to catch him up personally, and to share the vision we had been working on around Restore Katy. I scheduled a meeting with him for 4:00 PM that afternoon.

After being in the neighborhood for the last several days, it was even more apparent that we had to stay engaged in the recovery process. As Jerry had said that morning, "you can fake caring, but you can't fake showing up!" The Fellowship had shown up in amazing ways thus far for our neighbors impacted by Harvey, and we had an opportunity to continue showing up.

Jayson, David, and I had developed a vision and strategy for how we could continue assisting our neighbors through the restoration process. It was big, but The Fellowship had partnered with other churches to do big things in the past. We had already done some amazing things during Harvey in the rescue phase and we were pressing hard in the clean up phase as well (the first step towards Restoration).

RESTORE KATY

Vision - Through the power of Jesus facilitate the restoration of every home in the greater Katy area.

Mission:
1. Identify, procure, store, and deploy construction materials, equipment, and supplies needed for restoration.
2. Identify, onboard, deploy, and manage people doing restoration.
3. Do this all with a grassroots neighbor oriented structure that is HIGH touch for our neighbors who have been impacted (A Care Coordinator will take their hand and walk them all the way through the process). This will include a database that connected churches can access to adopt a neighbor in need.

We believed that, working with other churches and organizations (FEMA, insurance agencies, non-profits), we could insure that all the homes that were impacted in the greater Katy area (a community of approximately 300,000 people) were restored.

We knew there were certain "non-negotiables" we wanted to operate within, things that must be part of how we functioned. We identified these as values:

Key Values:
1. We want to keep the personal touch. As agencies take over during the various phases of a disaster, they become less neighborly and personal. We want to keep at the forefront the reality that these are our neighbors throughout the process. Our NEIGHBORS have been impacted mightily. To help us keep this focus, we will find emotionally intelligent, strong believing, Prayers in the church who will be the heart, eyes and ears of Jesus as others serve as His hands and feet!
2. We don't care who gets the credit!
3. We want our community rebuilt even better than it was!
4. We want to be decentralized, not centralized. We know we need structures and procedures but we want a flat organization that delivers care and recovery!
5. If someone is doing it better FOR OUR COMMUNITY we will let them run with it. Before we let them run with it we will first verify that they are truly doing it better. We won't just take their word for it, we want to see that they are doing it!
6. We don't want to become a relief agency. We are a Church . . . who wants to provide relief for our members and our community. Jesus has got to be central.
7. Resources are flowing through our community like crazy. We want to capture the ones that will help with recovery and ask for the right things from folks who are out of town.
8. Do I believe that God is big enough to accomplish this vision?
9. We are committed to using the resources we receive with integrity. In many disasters the people impacted by the disaster don't really get much tangible benefit. Many resources are stolen and wasted. We won't let this happen because we belong to Jesus and we truly want to help our neighbors.

We were already on our way towards fleshing out the structure to fulfill this vision. People had volunteered to fill key roles in this organizational chart going forward. Looking over this today, there are things I would change, like putting the Care Director as a direct report to the Executive Director. But overall, it works as a

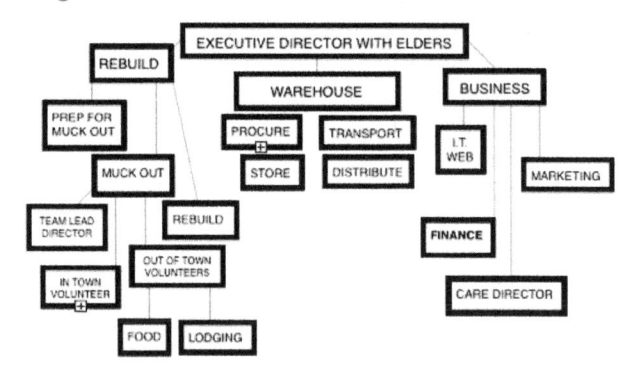

Mission Critical Issues:
1. a large volunteer base
2. resources to muck out homes and rebuild homes
3. a database of every person impacted in the greater Katy area

Restore Katy must run as a lean, "volunteer focused" organization. Hires will only be made when absolutely necessary and for key people. There are enough resources in the Kingdom of God to get this done!

simple flat organization.

We also developed job descriptions for the roles identified. Many of these would be filled by volunteers, and we knew that clarity of roles and expectations is as important with volunteers as it is with paid staff!

In business, working with volunteer organizations is a truly unique experience. Passion and story are the primary motivators, the "carrots" in the equation. In a "for pay" organization, these are also the BEST motivators. Often, however, monetary compensation is THE primary motivator in "for pay" businesses. . . . and it can be a strong one!

As we transitioned out of the "my house is flooded please come save me" phase of volunteering to the "I know you are busy back at work and with your family, but I need some help getting this sheetrock growing mold out of my home" phase, we knew passion and story would become even more vital to

JOB DESCRIPTIONS

Executive Director - Own and execute the vision. Must be able to build systems not just work within a system.

Assistant Director - Serve as the Executive Director when the Executive Director is out of town or unavailable.

Church Liaison - Actively recruit, resource, and serve churches accessing our shared database. This person will be the connection between churches serving the community and Restore Katy. They should be able to network well and involve others in networking and advocating for the organization.

Rebuild Director - Own the vision and execute around any and all aspects of the Prep for Muck Out, Muck Out and Rebuild process, current and anticipated in the future. Must be able to develop systems that maximize TOT (Time on Tools). Will insure that we are the hands and feet of Jesus (and that we do it with His heart as well).

Assistant Rebuild Director - Serve as the Rebuild Director when the Director is out of town or unavailable.

Prep For Muck Out Coordinator - Responsible for all aspects of getting Impacted Neighbor (IN) homes prepped for Muck Out. Be the contact between the Care Coordinator and the Prep For Muck Out Leader. Must be able to shoulder tap, train, and expand Prep For Muck Out Leaders.

Prep For Muck Out Leader - Leads a team to assist the IN in prep for Muck Out.

Muck Out Leader Coordinator - Develop a system for growing the number of Muck Out Team Leaders and insure they are trained and delivering Muck Outs efficiently, graciously, and within defined parameters. Be the contact between the Care Coordinator and the Muck Out Leader. Must be able to shoulder tap, train, and expand Muck Out Leaders.

Muck Out Leader - Leads a team to assist the IN in the Muck Out of their home.

In Town Volunteer Coordinator - Coordinates every aspect of mobilizing volunteers to participate in the rebuild process. Must be able to build and work within a system that is high touch and inspires volunteers to "give it all they got."

Out of Town Volunteer Coordinator - Coordinates every aspect of out of town teams. Must insure that people have a place to serve and know they are appreciated.

"Food for Out of Town Volunteers" Coordinator - Will coordinate food for the out of town volunteers with the Out of Town Volunteer Coordinator.

"Lodging for Out of Town Volunteers" Coordinator - Will coordinate lodging for the out of town volunteers with the Out of Town Volunteer Coordinator.

Rebuild Construction Coordinator - Will give leadership and direction to the rebuild of the IN home. Must be able to build systems and structures to insure this is accomplished with attention to detail and within code.

Warehouse Supervisor - Own the vision and execute around any and all supply needs, current and anticipated in the future. Must be able to build out the team around procuring, storing, transporting and distributing materials.

Assistant Warehouse Supervisor - Serve as the Warehouse Supervisor when the Supervisor is out of town or unavailable.

Business Manager - Own the vision and execute around any and all aspects of business operation, current and anticipated in the future. Must be able to build a system that supports the needs of the organization.

Assistant Business Manager - Serve as the Manager when the Manager is out of town or unavailable.

Care Coordinator Director - Will insure that our IN are not just a number in a system but that their hands are held throughout the process. The director will insure that Care Coordinators are resourced to be the heart, eyes, ears, and mouth of Jesus. Will also insure that the Care Coordinators are cared for through the process.

Care Coordinator - Be the initial and ongoing contact for our IN. Will cry with, pray with, and advocate for the rebuild of their home. They will work with the IN as if they are their Aunt, Uncle, or Grandparent who has been impacted. They will help the IN facilitate the restoration of their home (the IN must always be the leader in their restoration).

Finance Administrator - Will insure that we have systems and structures in place that financially resource our vision with integrity and simple systems.

Marketing Director - Will help develop a compelling face for the organization and the vision. Will insure that our communications are clear, compelling and Jesus centered.

IT / Web / DataBase Coordinator - This person will help Restore Katy be a computer based organization that communicates well within the organization and without. They will develop systems that are critical and user friendly. They will help insure the integrity of our data.

keeping a motivated volunteer base. At this point, we had organized an amazing number of volunteers in the rescue phase of recovery, truly serving as a lighthouse in our community. Why couldn't we do the same thing for the restoration process?

Everyone that we talked with about the demo phase of restoration said it was a seven to eight week process. After

Volunteer needs for the next 8 weeks that we know of:
People to make phone calls to volunteer list (with a script)
People to assist key people
People to help prep for muck out
People to help move people out of their apartment, home or rental
People to Muck Out
People to Care Coordinate
People to lead Muck Out
People to help with food for out of town volunteers
People to host home for out of town volunteers
People with trucks and SUV to move stuff

Process for rebuild:
Electric and plumbing
Insulation
Sheetrock - Tape/Float
Trim/Doors/Quarter Rounds
Cabinets
Countertops
Windows
Floors
Texture for walls
Paint (all trim, caulking and walls)

that amount of time, if nothing had been done, houses would be destroyed to the slab because of mold. We identified key volunteers we would need for the Demo Phase and included the steps we had identified for the Rebuild Phase of restoration. Jerry was very receptive, and asked me to continue working with Glenn on this over the next few weeks as I did what I could with my other duties at the church.

On Monday, September 11, school restarted for Katy ISD. It was a great day, being back in the normality of my role as classroom teacher. We wanted to ease back into things as much as possible. However, there was no way I could pass up the US History lesson around what we had just been through in responding to a tragedy, and what New York went through on 9/11.

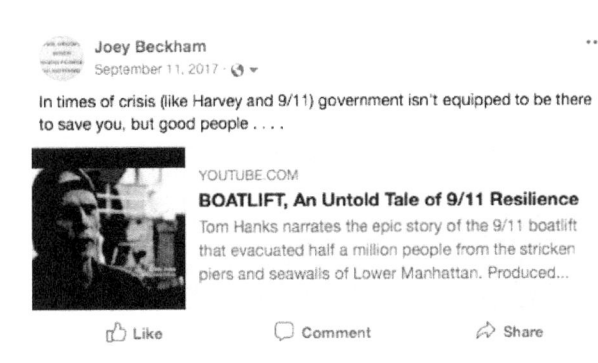

We dove back into some of the routine for our class, what we were going to do the rest of the semester, and how we would adjust for Harvey. We spent some time sharing what we had been through with Harvey, and I ended class by showing this amazing video about the boat lift rescues in New York. This rescue was organized by citizens on 9/11 and was the greatest single boat rescue operation in history, even greater than Dunkirk!

> **Joey Beckham**
> September 11, 2017
>
> In times of crisis (like Harvey and 9/11) government isn't equipped to be there to save you, but good people . . . .
>
> YOUTUBE.COM
> **BOATLIFT, An Untold Tale of 9/11 Resilience**
> Tom Hanks narrates the epic story of the 9/11 boatlift that evacuated half a million people from the stricken piers and seawalls of Lower Manhattan. Produced...
>
> Like   Comment   Share

> Transitioning back into my former life
>
> Joey Beckham
>
> Wayne S; Glenn L; Aaron G
>
> Good afternoon!
>
> Just wanted to let you know I'm in the process of transitioning back into my Groups Pastor role. I am available to Glenn on a "how can I help basis" for the next couple of weeks. I will be off ramping my contacts and work buddies towards you guys.
>
> We have had an awesome start at this . . . I'll be praying for you as you press hard to the finish line!
>
> Joey

After school, I swung by the neighborhoods to check on some folks we had helped the day before. I went by the church and sent an email out to the team to let them know I, like many of them, was getting back to a new "normal." None of us were sure what that looked like, but schools, jobs, life, and family were calling us back to reality.

The rest of the week was a blur of school, texts and calls from those we were helping, contacts from new people needing help, working with Glenn and others to transition my responsibilities, trying to get time with Connie,

The Fellowship
September 15, 2017

As we move into the Reconstruction Phase of our work following Hurricane Harvey, our needed donations have changed once again! If you are able to provide any of these materials please let us know! Thank you!

4' x 8' x 1/2" Sheetrock Need Donation Lots of 20 sheets, standard and mold resistant

Soquete Sheet Rock Mud
OR Joint Compound 18lb-25lb 45 or 90 minute variety

R13 or R19 Batt Insulation for 16 inch center studs

Pre-Hung Interior Doors 24", 30", 32" and 36"

Standard Refrigerators
Standard size stoves
Standard size Dishwashers
Range Tops - gas and electric

Camp chairs

and catching up on some of my lost sleep after averaging four or five hours for that last two weeks. I also worked closely with Carly, as she led our Care Coordinators, and with Jennifer, as she worked with our out of town volunteers. Community Beer and several others groups were still going strong, bringing teams of 12-15 every weekend. We put out a new needs list that reflected current reality.

Throughout the week, Glenn and Jerry began assuming more leadership for what we were doing and where we were headed. I transitioned into a support role for the next few months. Saturday, I took a much needed trip to Austin to hang out with our son Logan, and go to Pedernales Falls. He had come in one day during Harvey to help, but I hadn't seen him since then (and was pretty busy when he was in Katy).

On the way to Austin, I couldn't get away from the reminders of Harvey. Just north of Interstate 10 on Highway 71, there was an open field of about 200 acres that was being filled with flooded cars from Harvey. By the end of the day, tow truck after tow truck had driven there to unload one and often two cars they were towing. For the next couple of months, whenever I drove to Austin, it was a reminder of what we had been through.

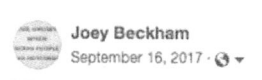

Joey Beckham
September 16, 2017

Must be the Harvey car graveyard on Hwy 71 near Columbus Texas. Crazy!

Leadership Lesson #34 - Leaders have a crystal clear understanding of what is within their control and what is NOT within their control. They expend little energy on things NOT within their control.

BACK TO NORMAL NORMAL

September 17 to November 17 - Harvey Normal to Normal Normal

For the next two months, real life and Harvey intermingled significantly. The weeks were a circus level act of juggling school, family, and Harvey. My "Harvey Normal" life was a blur of busyness, trying to maintain my pre-Harvey life as I also helped folks navigate through their recovery and restoration. During this time, I continued to live into the reality that sleep, food, free time, and football are overrated!

During the week of September 17, structures began to get developed at the church for our response. Impacted neighbors were moving forward in their recovery. Many were able to get into our system via the online fillable form. Ultimately, we had 277 homes on our master list, and we contacted each family. Those who needed our help were assigned Care Coordinators who walked with them through the process. We were being the heart of Christ to those impacted.

Our Demo Team Leader, Wayne, got demo teams organized to serve as the "hands and feet" of Christ. We had local volunteers coming in throughout the week that helped make progress on homes. We geared up for a significant response over the weekend, as out of town volunteers came to join our own volunteers in the neighborhoods. Jennifer worked closely with our out of town volunteers to coordinate their presence over the weekend, provide lodging, logistics, and food while they were here.

September 23, I was in the impacted portion of our community and amazed at how things still looked. Most of us were back to a semblance of our normal lives, with work and family, while our neighbors were still struggling to recover from the floods. Trash service had yet to be restored to most of the impacted neighborhoods.

Joey Beckham
September 23, 2017

This is today, 2 miles from the church I work at in Katy, Texas. Street after street after street. 700+ homes in this one subdivision and 85% of them without flood insurance.

Carly and I continued to work closely together as she led Care

Coordinators and I was available to get into the neighborhoods and organize teams. I also worked closely with Glenn and Wayne as they followed up with people impacted and organized demo crews. The weekend of September 23, along with an amazing volunteer sitting at our front desk, I helped call most of the people on our list who had not yet been contacted.

On September 24, we got an email from Glenn that church leadership had decided to allow the Texas Baptist Men and Kingsland Baptist to lead the reconstruction efforts. We would continue demoing and care coordinating, but we would pass rebuilding to them. Most impacted neighbors who were demoed were finding that FEMA and their insurance adjusters were very slow in getting the final approval on rebuilding their home.

Over the next couple of weeks, the warehouse began receiving donated supplies from all over the country. The outpouring of help and support was astounding!

My texts throughout these weeks are filled with "here is a new person to work with" and "did you follow up with _____?" and "alright, we are done with _____ home, who's next?" and "Hi, Joey, my name is _____ we talked about getting help for _____."

From almost the first day of demoing, I networked with Todd, an amazing contact from Hope City Church. He was helping folks like crazy as he was trying to get his rent home restored from the flood! John and I went by to give him a hand one night, putting sheetrock up in his rent house. He was a great encouragement throughout the whole process!

In the midst of all this, Connie and Carly took a much needed trip to Nashville for a Christian Counselors conference the weekend of September 29. At a local park, John and I got some quality time with nieces and nephews while they were out of town. Hundreds of neighbors were out enjoying the day. I couldn't help but think of the thousands of neighbors, within a few miles of us in every direction, who were still struggling to recover.

96

The organized response was coming together and Omar, the Missions Pastor who had been working tirelessly with his team at Kingsland Baptist, further developed Katy Disaster Response. Their online presence was a great place for people to self-identify and find needed information and help.

The weekend of September 30, I continued coordinating crews through The Fellowship, but had the awesome opportunity to work with my colleagues at McMeans helping a couple of our former students and their family. They lived near the school and had been flooded in their home by about six inches. They had demoed as they could, but needed help. As we evaluated their situation, we determined that they would need to take out their hardwood floors, despite the minimal amount of water they had in the home. That was back breaking work! Floated hardwood floors were fairly easy, but glued hardwood floors were taken out after an inch by inch battle! Some of our Community Beer guys showed up, so we ended up with a crew of about eighteen. It took a backbreaking three hours with "all hands on deck" to take up the 1,000 square foot or so of hardwood floors. This agonizing experience was being reproduced all over Katy!

I was in a neighborhood the weekend of October 7 where I took pictures of "The Claw" showing up to pick up the first floor trash pile in front of flooded homes. For homeowners, this was a long-awaited phenomenon. It was a very visual step towards normalcy. Getting the trash picked up opened the door for impacted neighbors to begin cleaning up their yard and doing landscaping, another big step away from the memory of Harvey.

While I was waiting to drive around the claw truck blocking the road, we parked and looked for a place to help. We ended up in the home of one of those flooded in the neighborhood. The homeowner took me into the bedroom and showed his handiwork to preserve his outside brick wall. When the flood happened, the swollen wood and walls pushed the brick veneer on the home almost off the slab! He installed an anchor in the concrete floor and an intricate tension system with "come alongs" to save the wall and bring it back in. It was amazing to see the ingenuity of people in times of need!

Later that day, I found myself in a home who had reached out to us needing their tile floor taken out. John, myself, the homeowner, and her son spent several hours over Saturday and Sunday working with sledge hammers and long pry bars to get that floor up. On the way out of the home on Sunday, I met her next door neighbor. He was one of my kids' coaches when they were in high school! He had been impacted as well.

On October 12, several of us received an awesome email from one of our Care Coordinators. Their job had truly been a ministry of love as they walked alongside impacted neighbors. These neighbors often became like family. She very graciously shared that she understood our shift in focus away from restoration, but lovingly petitioned us to help one of her families in desperate need. She was concerned they would fall through the cracks as they were passed off to "someone else" at another church to care for them. Our vision to be the heart of Christ as we were His hands and feet had blossomed!

The next few weeks, things slowed considerably for me around Harvey. I was much more engaged in my pre-Harvey life, with periodic interruptions to help those recovering from Harvey. On November 17, I officially shaved the Harvey Beard. My first day back at McMeans way back in September people asked me about my new look and I told them it was my Harvey Beard. Like baseball players often do during the playoffs, it was my own personal reminder that despite appearances, things were not "business as usual." As I initially got engaged with Harvey, NOT shaving became a visual reminder to me that I had neighbors around me who were suffering. I knew how easy it would be for me, someone not directly impacted, to go back to my life with minimal residual interruption from Harvey. Every morning when I got up and looked in the mirror, I was reminded that my friends were not back to normal . . . . yet. I know it sounds simple, but my Harvey Beard gave me a sense of urgency about being engaged in helping those in need all around me.

After November 17, I returned to normal normal. Sure, I have stayed in touch with many of my Harvey Friends. We have kept up with each other on social media and via text. I celebrated with Robert when he got in his home. I even performed a renewal of wedding vows for Audrey and her husband!

Others have taken the baton of restoration and run with it.

Over the last few months, Joel Davidson and Tom Pretti have developed Katy Responds. Joel was personally impacted by Harvey and got involved with The Fellowship in our response as soon as possible. He eventually ran our warehouse and worked intimately with demo crews and many of our out of town volunteers. Tom was vitally involved around Harvey from the beginning, as the local Missions Coordinator for Grace Fellowship. Tom and Joel have developed an organization to bring together churches across the Katy area to help finish the restoration of homes. Currently, of the 14,000 homes impacted in the six greater Katy zip codes, there are approximately 2,000 that have not rebuilt. For example, in Canyon Gate, where we helped a lot, there were 721 homes that flooded with 180 still needing help today. Joel and Tom's vision is to rebuild 100 unfinished homes and then work from there. For more information on this organization, you can go to their website: katyresponds.org.

For those of us who live in the Houston area, the threat of a massive hurricane is an annual experience. Harvey has definitely made the danger more tangible and palpable. Yesterday, I took this picture of crews out preparing the drainage ditches around my neighborhood, a stark reminder that hurricane season is fast approaching. To date, nothing extensive has been done to address the potentiality of the reservoirs overflowing again. Another example of the snail's pace response of government.

Thankfully, if we do have another catastrophic hurricane, I am more confident today than ever before, that there are tens of thousands of men and women across this great state and across the country who will respond. Ordinary men and women, who will do extraordinary things, if the need should ever present itself again.

Leadership Lesson #35 - Leaders insure the right people are on the bus and in the right seat on the bus. They know some people will push the vision forward and some will slow vision progression to a crawl.

Dedication and Acknowledgements

Wednesday - July 18, 2018

First and foremost, I want to acknowledge a good God who loves us through the storms of life. Yes, storms will come, but He is present with us through them. If you don't interact with Jesus Christ on a daily basis, I encourage you to get to know Him. He is an amazing Savior and Friend to anyone who needs one.

My family sacrificed a lot for me to help with Harvey and write this book. Connie, I love you, you are an amazing woman of God. Carly, Logan, and John, I love you with all my heart. It is a joy to see your hearts of compassion and care for others.

My parents and grandparents gave me a lot of love and taught me the joy of giving and of hard work and dedication. I have a blessed heritage and legacy!

The Fellowship church family is an amazing example of people dedicated to living their relationship with Jesus Christ through words and deeds. What you did during Harvey is a shining example for any other church who finds itself in the midst of a disaster.

Katy ISD, Dr. Hindt, and the school board truly were a blessing to this community during Harvey. They did so much to respond and make things better for their city. I am very proud to be a part of this organization.

I want to celebrate the heart and grit of my neighbors who were impacted. They dove in and have worked hard to recover from their tragedy. I don't believe that in all the interactions I had with impacted neighbors did I find anyone not giving all they had to facilitate their own recovery.

To every person who did anything they could to ease the pain of another during this disaster I say, "WELL DONE!" So many of us did what we could without expectation. We shuttled people around, hosted people in our homes, took in friends, prepared meals, washed clothes, risked our lives in boats out in flood waters, hauled trash to the curb, donated money, demoed houses, helped rebuild homes, cried with our neighbors, entered into the pain of another. This was truly inspirational to experience.

To government employees, National Guard, First Responders, Sheriff and law enforcement who walked alongside us in the rescue and restoration, your sacrifice and service does not go unnoticed. We know the risks you take every day to serve your community. We recognize the time you spend away from your family to protect our families. You are much appreciated!

As I tell this story, I don't in any way want to diminish what thousands and thousands of people from Katy and all over the country did to help during this catastrophe. During this response to Harvey, I saw many Heroes. In my mind, a Hero is anyone who shows up in a crisis and tries to leverage the influence they have to make the situation better. During Harvey, we had thousand of Heroes working throughout this recovery effort. Some are still working today!

I want to acknowledge the hundreds of people I personally encountered, who were helping in all kinds of ways, whom I did not mention by name in this book. You know who you are! My memory is fading, but what you did will not quickly be forgotten by those you impacted.

Writing this book has been an awesome opportunity for me to relive an incredibly unique experience in my life. I have shed some tears as I have written and remembered. That is a good thing. As you finish this book, I hope it helps you do a few things:

I hope it helps you process through your grief and your Harvey experience.

I hope this book encourages you to NOT sit around and wait on someone else to help you in a disaster. The calvary isn't coming, YOU are the calvary.

I hope it inspires you to do whatever you can to ease the pain and suffering of others.

I hope it gives those who specifically encounter a water-related disaster some tools to respond and a sense of how things progress.

I hope that for anyone who gets involved in helping out in a flood, at any stage from Rescue to Restoration, it gives you insight so you can avoid some of the mistakes we made.

Finally, I hope no one feels shame or guilt for what they didn't do or think they should have done. One of my favorite verses in the Bible is, "there is, therefore, now no condemnation for those who are in Christ Jesus." The Devil is all about shame and condemnation, Jesus came to bring LIFE, Hope, Healing and Freedom!

I would love to continue interacting with you as you process through your Harvey Experience. I have created a public Facebook group called, "Hurricane Harvey: Rescue to Restoration." If you would like to share a comment or story, that would be awesome. If you have pictures or videos you would like to post, I'd love to see them. Like me, you may find that talking about your experience is a very healing thing to do.

South of I-10 is Barker Reservoir, fed by Mason Creek and upper Buffalo Bayou from the Katy Prairie, its origin, and continues toward downtown.

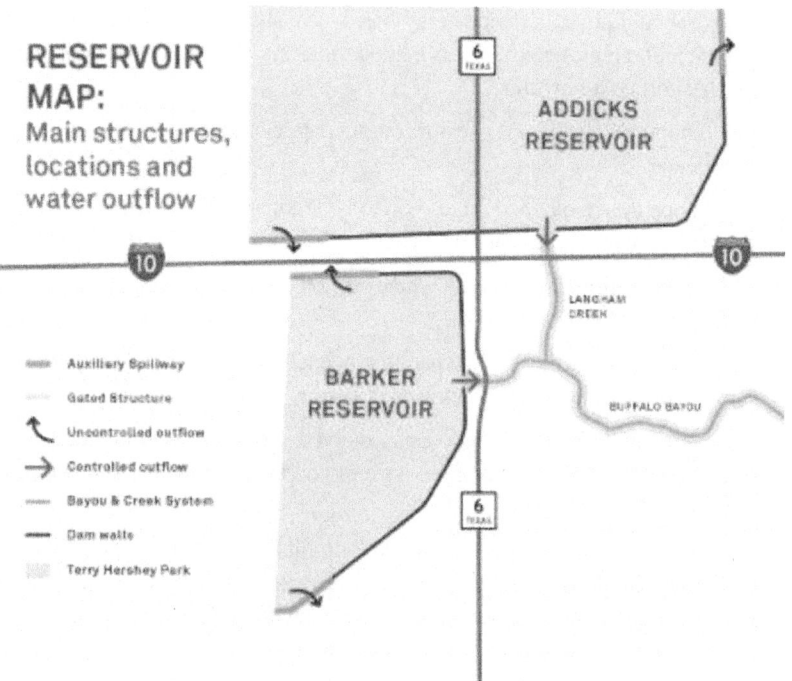

RESERVOIR MAP:
Main structures, locations and water outflow

- Auxiliary Spillway
- Gated Structure
- Uncontrolled outflow
- Controlled outflow
- Bayou & Creek System
- Dam walls
- Terry Hershey Park

Image: Evan O'Neil.

Long explained that the reservoirs have three main structural components. There are earthen embankments, which are the highest walls. The embankments are 121 feet high at Addicks and 112 feet at Barker.

Each reservoir also has a "gated water control structure," or flood gate. It works like a heart valve, able to be opened and closed.

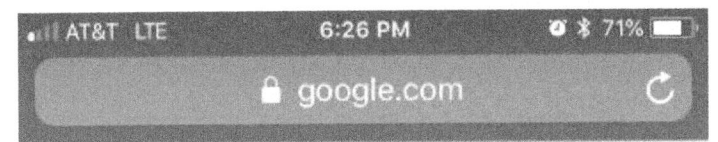

The two resevoirs were built after devastating floods in 1929 and 1935, and were designed to hold water until it can be released downstream at a controlled rate.

In Houston's southwestern suburbs, officials in Fort Bend County, Texas, warned Tuesday the Brazos River is projected to crest at 59 feet, FOX 26 Houston reported.

The Fort Bend County Office of Emergency Management issued a new advisory Tuesday warning subdivisions where residents should prepare to be affected by the floodwaters.

With nearly two more feet of rain expected on top of the 30-plus inches in some places, authorities worried the worst might be yet to come from Harvey. As of Tuesday, at least 14 people have died in the historic storm, including a family of six trying to escape the floodwaters, authorities said.

"We know in these kind of events that, sadly, the death toll goes up historically," Houston

https://www.nytimes.com/interactive/2018/03/22/us/houston-harvey-flooding-reservoir.html

https://www.nytimes.com/2018/03/19/us/harvey-texas-flooding.html

"We can hold approximately a 100-year-flood within the boundaries of the government property," Long explained. "People have built on the land that is above the government property, but below the max possible pool level the dams can hold."

In short, the capacity of the dam is beyond the government property, and the Army Corps is handling a very complex emergency situation by controlling high-volume releases to protect the city as a whole.

"It has never flooded before above the property," Long said. "This is the first time we have flooded homes located adjacent to and upstream from the property."

If more water from upstream enters the reservoirs, the water level will continue to rise. If the inflow and outflow match, the water is level. If the inflow is less than the outflow, the water level will start to fall.

Long, who has worked with the Army Corps for 36 years, unknowingly predicted this perfect storm that has sent so many along the Gulf Coast scrambling for dry land, safety and shelter. In the span of a week, Houston has shown the rest of America and the world what it is made of.

The city has come together in collective grief while maintaining its indomitable spirit. More than 50 people have died. But teams with inflatable boats and human chains have rescued those trapped amid swirling waters and many volunteers are sending surplus supplies to Beaumont and other ravaged communities. The storm is challenging us to co-exist with our watersheds, creeks, streams and, most importantly, Buffalo Bayou. Managing flooding is our city's greatest challenge and biggest opportunity.

Editor's note: This article was produced in collaboration with the Houston Chronicle.

And each reservoir has two auxiliary spillways. The spillways at Addicks are 111.5 feet high, and they are 105 feet high at Barker. They are designed to back up the gated structures and work like the overflow holes in a sink, keeping water from going over the top or "overtopping" the embankments.

"We have designed the dams so that, in an extreme event larger the Harvey, water will go over the auxiliary spillway and never over the main embankment," he said. "The dams are prepared for events beyond what we are experiencing right now."

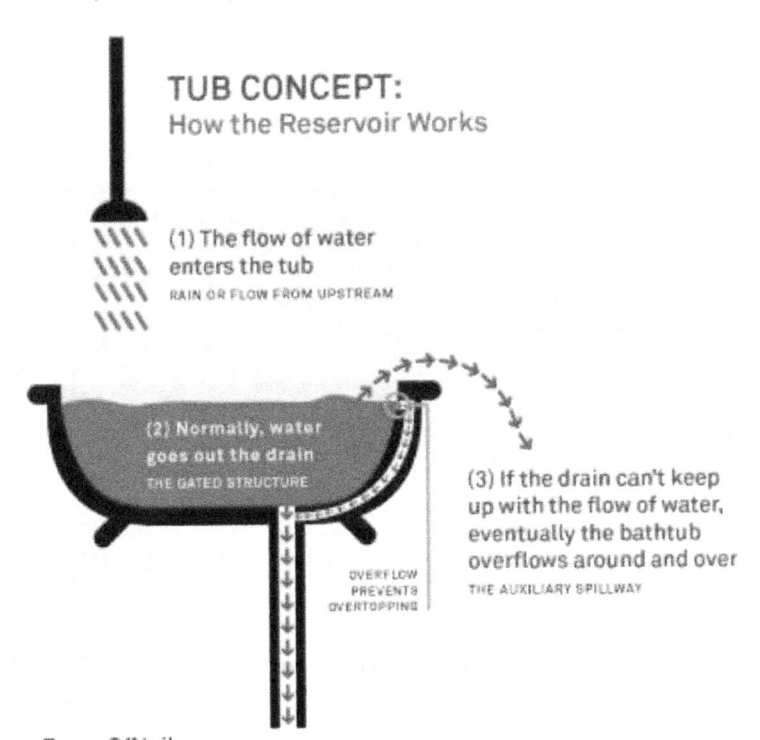

TUB CONCEPT:
How the Reservoir Works

(1) The flow of water enters the tub
RAIN OR FLOW FROM UPSTREAM

(2) Normally, water goes out the drain
THE GATED STRUCTURE

OVERFLOW PREVENTS OVERTOPPING

(3) If the drain can't keep up with the flow of water, eventually the bathtub overflows around and over
THE AUXILIARY SPILLWAY

ige: Evan O'Neil.

One other part of this that I found fascinating was that the Army Corps of Engineers was basically powerless to do more. My understanding is that water was coming in to the Addicks at aboue 40,000 cu ft/hr for days, while the max controlled outflow is only about 7,000 cubic feet/hr. In other words, had they opened the dam to max outflow a full day before they did any releases, it only would've cleared about 4.2 hours worth of inflow (7k*24 = 168k; 40k*4 = 160k), meaning the uncontrolled release over the spillway still would've happened, just 4 hours later. (Assuming my inflow numbers are right, and that that rate was maintained over the relevant time period).

Does the dam have other overflow spillways between 108ft and 121ft? Clearly the flow rate out the 108ft spillway wasn't enough to match the inflow rate (because the water kept rising above 108ft), which means it's theoretically possible to overtop the main dam. Hopefully there are other "relief valves" that

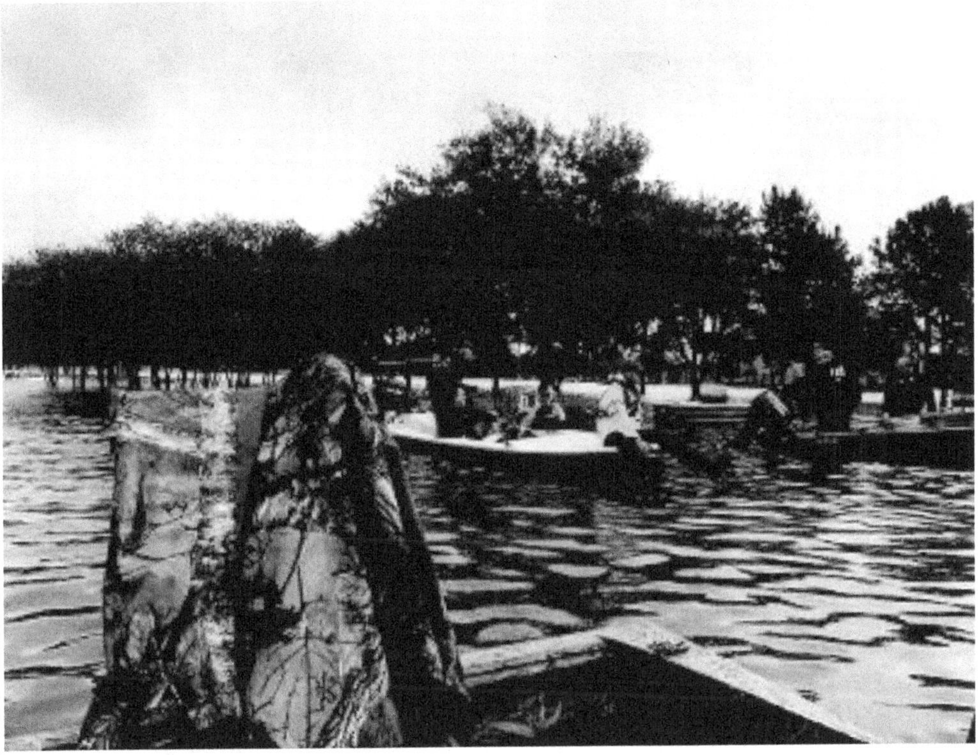

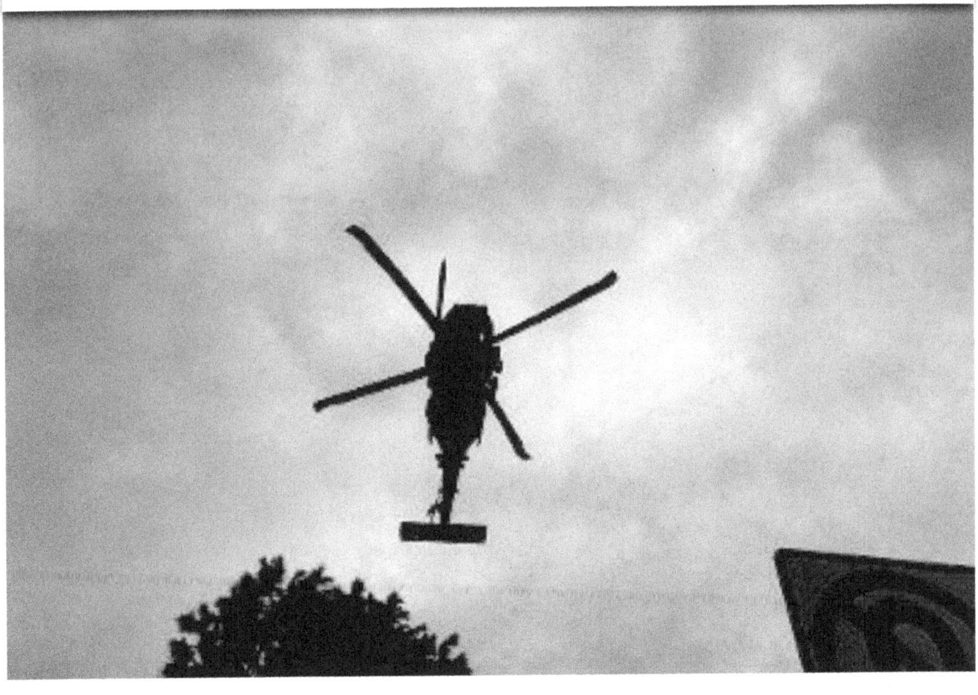

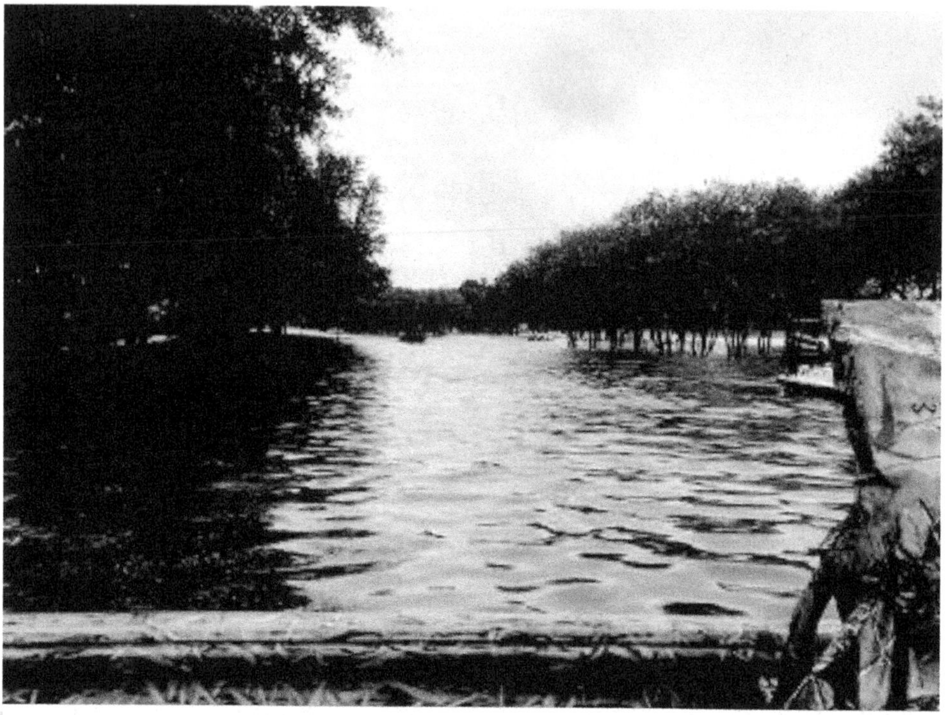

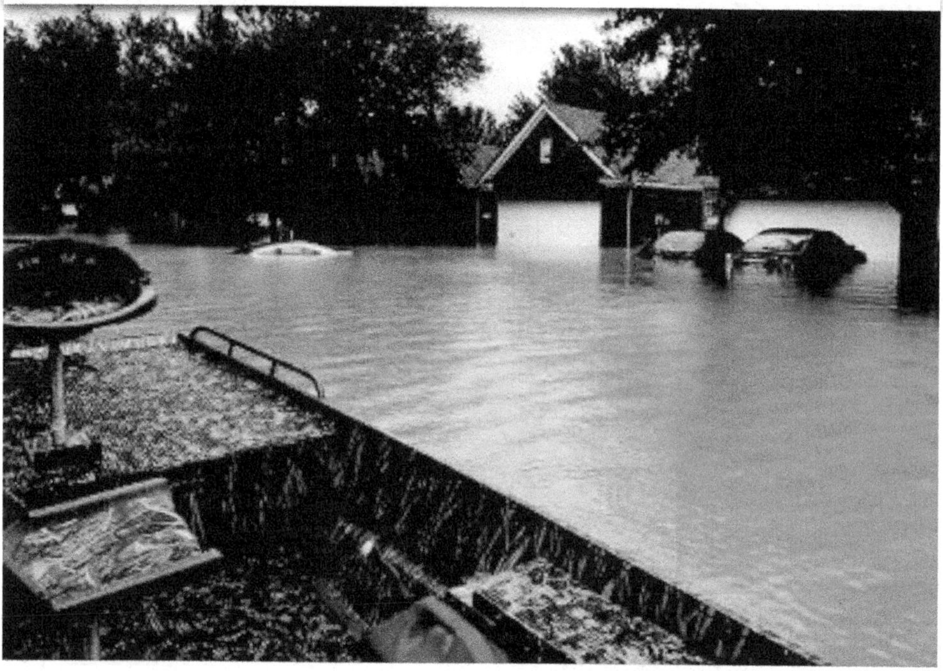

Made in the USA
Columbia, SC
27 August 2018